International Women in Design

To My Mom . . .

Thanks to all the designers' who
contributed their work. To Dianne,
Linda, and Wayne, for assuring the
project's smooth completion.
And to Jerry McConnell, who
saw the need for this book
and the good it could do.

— *Supon Phornirunlit*

ISBN: 0-942604-30-X
Library of Congress Catalog Card Number: 92-061448

Distributed to the trade in the United States and Canada by :
Van Nostrand Reinhold
115 Fifth Avenue
New York, NY 10003

Distributed throughout the rest of the world by:
Hearst Books International
105 Madison Avenue
New York, NY 10016

Published by:
Madison Square Press
10 East 23rd Street
New York, NY 10010

International Women in Design is a project of:

Supon Design Group, Inc.,
International Book Division
1000 Connecticut Avenue, NW
Suite 415
Washington, DC 20036

Printed in Hong Kong

International Women in Design

SUPON DESIGN GROUP

ACKNOWLEDGMENTS

Project Director: Supon Phornirunlit

Communications Director: Wayne Kurie

Art Director: Supon Phornirunlit

Project Manager: Dianne S. Cook

Managing Editor: Wayne Kurie

Book Designer: Dianne S. Cook

Cover Design: Richard Lee Heffner

Writers: Linda Klinger and Wayne Kurie

Production Artists: Andrew Berman, Angela K. Jackson, Rebecca A. Lepkowski, and Jennifer A. Lowe

Desktop Publisher: CompuPrint, Washington, D.C., USA

German Translator: Hans Treupel, with Petra Treupel

THANK YOU'S

Stuart Ash, Gottschalk+Ash International, Toronto, Ontario, Canada

Laurel Harper, *How Magazine*, Cincinnati, Ohio, USA

Barbara J. Murray, *Studio Magazine*, Toronto, Ontario, Canada

Tor Pettersen, Tor Pettersen & Partners, London, England

Lori Siebert, Siebert Design Associates, Cincinnati, Ohio, USA

TABLE OF CONTENTS

Introduction vi

Designers

Madeleine Bennett, *London, England* 2

Bethany Bunnell, *Hong Kong, Hong Kong* 10

Margo Chase, *Los Angeles, California, USA* 18

Sheila Levrant de Bretteville, *New Haven, Connecticut, USA* 26

Anna Eymont, *Paddington, New South Wales, Australia* 34

April Greiman, *Los Angeles, California, USA* 42

Catherine Haughton, *Toronto, Ontario, Canada* 50

Jane Hope, *Montreal, Quebec, Canada* 58

Diti Katona, *Toronto, Ontario, Canada* 66

Siobhan Keaney, *London, England* 74

Judy Kirpich, *Alexandria, Virginia, USA* 82

Sonsoles Llorens, *Barcelona, Spain* 90

Nora Olgyay, *Washington, D.C., USA* 98

Paula Scher, *New York, New York, USA* 106

Ellen Shapiro, *New York, New York, USA* 114

Lori Siebert, *Cincinnati, Ohio, USA* 122

Catherine Lam Siu-hung, *Hong Kong, Hong Kong* 130

Leslie Smolan, *New York, New York, USA* 138

Deborah Sussman, *Culver City, California, USA* 146

Rosmarie Tissi, *Zurich, Switzerland* 154

Lynn Trickett, *London, England* 162

Susanna Vallebona, *Milan, Italy* 170

Nancy Williams, *London, England* 178

Project Credits 187

Selection Process 197

About Supon Design Group 198

Introduction

When we decided to write International Women in Design, we were cautioned about the implications of producing a book that was gender-specific. Although some would see it for what it was — a compilation of outstanding design and the personal insights of the creators — we were assured others would question our motivations. Why "women" in design? Our reasons were simple: to recognize some talented people, to educate about the scope of work being produced, and, perhaps, to make a small stride forward in affording women more visibility in our industry.

We at Supon Design Group have long observed how women still struggle to be recognized in society. We'd also become somewhat weary of the way in which women's accomplishments are often portrayed. Filmmakers, authors and talk show hosts make a career out of emphasizing women's differences from men.

"From day one, I did what I wanted to in design. I'm totally spoiled."

— Siobhan Keaney

But we didn't want another book that polarizes people. Instead, we wanted to laud the efforts of a population linked by gender, interest and success, without the need to compare them to anyone else. We hope this book heralds unity. International Women in Design celebrates a few people we have come to admire, who are as different from each other in goals, lifestyles and philosophies as — well, as one success story is different from another.

The graphics industry itself is still evolving. This book contains many surprises within the wide range of work this evolution has produced. Design's function — however noble — must first sell a product or service, or fail. The marriage of this ability to sell with true craft is an honorable skill. But there is also an art element of graphic design that offers silently stunning contributions to global aesthetics, continuity and communications. It is no surprise that most all these designers have experimented with some other form of craft or media — painting, etching, sculpture, writing — to refine their work in commercial art. Their creativity would stagnate without continual stimuli from without, or within.

What we learned in compiling this book, however, was not limited to design. We discovered a strong movement in the industry to address social responsibility — to make a difference. Nora Olgyay, for example, told us she looks at effective design as a service to the public. "I have a sincere desire," she said, "to explore ways to humanize the world — to make the world responsive to human needs." Olgyay supports the philosophy of legislation making public space more available to people with disabilities, especially that which applies to built environments — her specialty. Her design shows how she has met her goal.

"The easiest thing about being a designer is cleaning your desk before starting a project."

— *Anna Eymont*

Sheila Levrant de Bretteville concurs with Olgyay's beliefs. "My work is a graphic manifestation of social, political and humanistic expression," she says, and skeptics need only study her work to see its impact, and its ability to motivate, celebrate or heal. And from all, we learned to ignore cynics who tell designers "it can't be done," and found a definition for determination therein.

There is a great diversity of craft that makes up our industry. Catherine Haughton summed it up for us: "There is an element of style and fashion to what we do." But marketing remains an important element. Anna Eymont underscored the importance of letting the business world know what you're doing. Said Eymont, "I have always been an opportunist. I think you hold yourself back if you don't promote yourself and your accomplishments."

We discovered some people who excelled at the business of business, like Judy Kirpich, and those like Siobhan Keaney, who have never written a promotional brochure. Readers will encounter radically different design — just compare Margo Chase's fiercely complex concepts with Lori Siebert's playful use of color. Or Cat Lam's simple, bold lines and Paula Scher's quirky sense of humor. Some of these artists design behind closed doors, others work as an integral part of a team. One designs with music; another, without shoes.

Putting together a book of visions that spans four continents was an adventure. Happily, we were able to transcend time zones and overcome schedule discrepancies. There was a collective effort to overcome language barriers.

> **"I dream of making myself and others into heroines and heroes."**
> — *Sheila Levrant de Bretteville*

By exploring the portfolios and the brief thoughts of these individuals, many of whom are recognized throughout the world, we hope you'll achieve an insight into their motivations and goals, an accurate reflection of their careers and their lives, and an idea of how they got to where they are now.

As you read this book, consider it a snapshot that is all the more valuable for having frozen a time when these people were truly some of the best in the business. Remember that we learn much from history. These women have earned a place in the evolution of graphics, and their artwork beautifully tells the story. Keep your eye on them; we think their best work has yet to be created.

— *Supon Design Group*

Designers and Their Work

MADELEINE BENNETT

Madeleine Bennett Design
London, England

Ask Madeleine Bennett what comes after Madeleine Bennett Design, and she'll predict that any new venture won't differ much from what she does now. "I'll always be designing in one form or another, although someday I might concentrate on making more jewelry," she says, a craft she took up because she found it relaxing. "I'd like to make gold and silver pieces that are modern and spare, with a bit of wit to them. But design is so enjoyable, I don't think I'll ever want to stop doing that."

Packaging and advertisement for Giorgio Armani eyewear.

Packaging and logo application for Penhaligon's, a perfumerie.

Like the process of creating jewelry, Bennett likes to pare design work down to its core thought and build on it. This technique has won her two Clio Awards for menswear and eyewear packaging and four Silver Design and Art Direction Awards, among others. The solution, she says, comes from the problem — its audience, age group, market. "I like to take the problem apart and put it back together. The idea alone isn't enough — one has to make it work all the way through."

MADELEINE BENNETT

Brand identity and packaging for Classicus pens, Plus Corporation.

She calls her style varied, and her way of thinking logical. Bennett has developed a reliable track record with her clients "through hard work." "I don't think you achieve anything easily in life," she says. "I have a commitment to delivering a job on time and I set consistently high standards. But work is not a grind. It's easy to stay with design because it's great fun." For Bennett, drawing and painting all day long at Ravensbourne College of Art & Design was the definition of bliss. "I experienced fine arts, photography, screen printing, even pottery. Then I realized I could get paid for it," she says. She worked for the international graphics firm Pentagram and was on the Board of Directors of Michael Peters & Partners before opening her own studio.

Packaging for Free & Free, a brand of hair care products by Lion Corporation.

Brochure and identity for International Coffee Organisation, trade association.

Label design for a line of gourmet preserves by Elsenham Foods.

She defines design as an extremely powerful strategic business tool, but laughs when asked to summarize her process of design. "It's difficult to answer that," she admits, "because what you're asking is, how do I think? I suppose I conceptualize as to what would make sense, and then fit images and type together to create the approach. It's a good feeling to know I have skills other people find valuable — that I have something to offer."

MADELEINE BENNETT

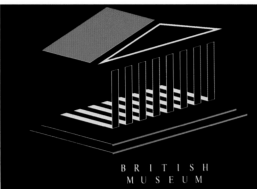

Bennett has a few words of wisdom for someone considering a career in graphics. "Get yourself into the best art school you can find," she advises. "Absorb as much as you can. You never really know until you've left art school how much fun you can have there — you have great opportunities to try new techniques and lots of equipment available." With 25 years in design, Bennett wistfully recalls the days when the industry was young and she was freer to experiment. "It seems much more difficult to be successful if you are just entering the business today. Competition is much greater."

Identity and related packaging for The British Museum Shop.

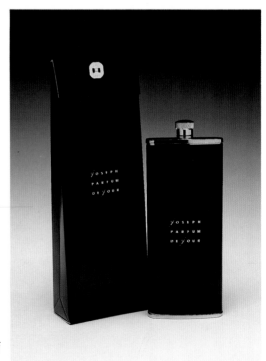

Packaging for the fragrances of Joseph, Parfum de Jour.

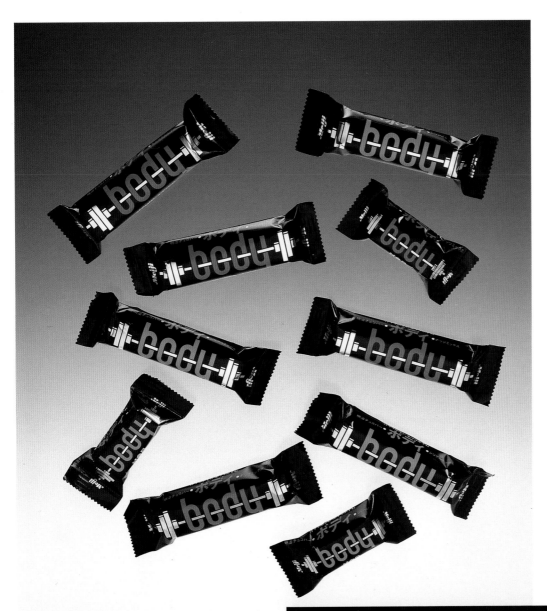

"Design is also becoming global," she notes. "You must be very aware of what's going on in the world. Design we haven't seen before is coming up from places like eastern Europe, an interesting source of indigenous artwork. The Spanish had not been a strong presence in design, but they did amazing things at the 1992 Olympics." Bennett herself produced an award-winning sports poster for the summer games. But growing world unity isn't all for the good, says Bennett, whose clients have included firms in Japan and the Middle East. "Part of the enjoyment of going to other countries is finding what they do differently. We're losing that. Special characteristics are becoming homogenized."

Identity for Body Bar, a chocolate snack aimed at young, health-conscious Japanese men.

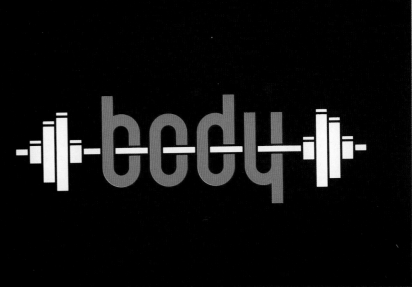

MADELEINE BENNETT

Although she's enjoying the challenge of company ownership, in the future Bennett hopes to join with other like-minded people and form a small studio partnership. "A large company is too impersonal for me," she says, having already worked for two big international firms. "Because corporations must be concerned primarily with the bottom line, they often do not leave much room for creative thought."

Graphic art, she believes, is a career ideally suited to the interests of most women. "Detailing, and the care and attention to colors and textures, are characteristics many women find fascinating. These skills are valuable in this kind of business. These same interests must have produced some excellent women painters and musicians over the centuries, who were not known because of the lesser positions of women in society in the past. I appreciate the fact that things have changed."

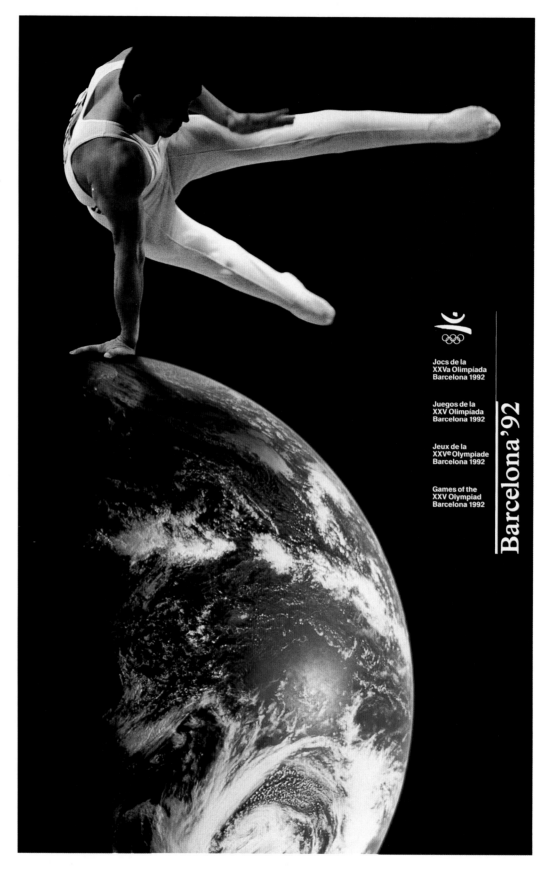

Jocs de la
XXVa Olimpíada
Barcelona 1992

Juegos de la
XXV Olimpiada
Barcelona 1992

Jeux de la
XXVe Olympiade
Barcelona 1992

Games of the
XXV Olympiad
Barcelona 1992

Barcelona '92

*Several of 28 posters for the
1992 Olympic Games
in Barcelona, Spain.*

BETHANY BUNNELL

STAR-TV
Hong Kong, Hong Kong

Joining the professional practice program at the University of Cincinnati was one of Bethany Bunnell's best career moves to date. Settling in Hong Kong — a place she'd never even visited before — was another. "It was a challenge. It forced me to wear different hats and to continue to grow," says the Virginia Beach, Virginia native. "I believe you should take chances and work where you can learn something new. Don't stay comfortable. Once you stop learning, it is time to move on."

Invitation and announcement for Bunnell's wedding.

Dear,

Robert

We will be married on Saturday 29 December, 1990 at two o'clock at Carol and Jerry's home.

We would be so happy if you would join us for the ceremony and the celebration to follow.

Love,

Bethany and Mark

MTV: Music Television on STAR TV brings you the latest music

and pop culture from Asia and around the world: live concerts,

exclusive interviews, music news and outrageous contests.

One of a series of MTV in Asia *posters done to promote the five* STAR TV *channels.*

Her studio, Bunnell Design, had been in existence for less than six months when she was approached by Satellite Television Asian Region (STAR TV), the first pan-Asian satellite broadcaster. She is now design director at the station, which broadcasts to a potential market of over 2.6 billion people — more than half the world's population. "Success happens because of hard work, perseverance, adaptability and creative solutions. In Hong Kong, we often work 5 1/2-day weeks, 12-hour days."

The Far East has been a good location for the organized and pragmatic Bunnell. "I have always delivered on my promises. I have never let anyone down," she says, claiming her primary motivation is responsibility. The more responsibility she has, the more freedom in creating the solution. She excels at setting personal goals and achieving them. She skis, scuba dives, runs. She trained for the Macleohose Trail, a 100 km walk that covers several Hong Kong mountain peaks and has been equated with climbing Everest one and one-half times. She wants to complete the walk in less than 24 hours. Physical activity, she says, helps her manage stress.

BETHANY BUNNELL

*Bamboo logo for
MTV in Asia.*

"The research and initial
brainstorming make up for the
hard parts of my job. I always
wish I had the time and
resources to develop more
than two or three directions.
My most favorite part of
design is when I've created
something that surprises me
and when elements come
together to create a most
successful result — as we all
call it, a happy accident."

*Levis/MTV
limited-edition jeans jacket.*

Press kit for MTV.

Invitation for the 1992
MTV Video Music Awards.

"Use of computers is an integral part of my design process," asserts Bunnell. When she researches a project, she considers the visual as well as the positioning factors. "I think about the broader ramifications of the project. Can it benefit anyone else in the company? Can I use the elements created in other pieces for the project? Sometimes it is unnecessary to reinvent the wheel, and adapting existing components can create a new, unique piece. This addresses both our efficiency and our severe time limitations."

BETHANY BUNNELL

Graphic art was not her first choice. "I have always loved arts and crafts, from papier mâché to batik to knitting. Throughout high school, I wanted to be an architect. I loved math and art. During my senior year of high school, I took a career placement test, and the results indicated that I should be a mechanical engineer. So I enrolled in mechanical engineering at the University of Colorado. It lasted only one semester. By the second semester, I had enrolled in Figure Drawing and art classes. I was back in my element."

Bunnell practices what she believes is a good philosophy of design. "I think the design industry must become more sensitive to certain issues, such as environmental concerns, increased competition in the marketplace and the recession. For the industry to grow, we must be more aware of market demands and client sensitivities. Clients need effective solutions that achieve tangible results, such as increased product sales.

Identity and stationery for STAR TV.

Event banners for STAR TV Laser Show, organized to promote AIDS awareness.

Tickets, program, and sweatshirt.

Event graphics.

We need improved global awareness — more of a recognition of design produced by cultures outside the U.S., Japan and Europe. We need to learn how to better communicate with the business community. If a new logo does nothing to change the perception or attitudes of the company, no matter how many awards the design has received, it cannot be deemed successful."

BETHANY BUNNELL

Bunnell strives for a balanced life, for being happy both personally and professionally. "The two ideas are codependent. I believe you have to pay your dues to be successful. But by working hard, I can afford to travel and enjoy my personal life with my husband. I am fortunate that he is understanding and supportive."

Corporate identity and stationery for The Tomson Group, property developer and investor.

三光行企業團
Sun Moon Star

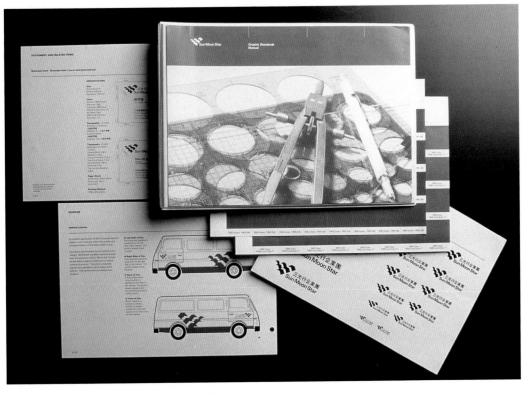

Identity manual for Sun Moon Star Corporation.

She's an adventurer. "Experiences are more important to me than actual possessions, although I do collect unusual objects from other cultures, like hand-painted rice fans and wedding hats from Vietnam, a stone statue from Indonesia and Burmese trading beads." Her Hong Kong experience has been well worth it, although she's curious about what will happen when Hong Kong reverts to Chinese leadership in 1997. There is the possibility of significant changes. But perhaps, she says, she will have moved on by then, tackling new challenges. There is still much to see.

MARGO CHASE

Margo Chase Design
Los Angeles, California, USA

Encountering Margo Chase's dramatic work in a record store can be startling. "Unlike conservative corporate accounts, the recording industry wants the trendiest and most radical art to portray their performers," says Chase, who can claim industry giants Warner Brothers, Virgin, Capitol, Geffen and MCA Records as clients. Her album cover concepts for artists like Prince, Madonna, Cher and Bonnie Raitt are created from a myriad of components: the musician, the audience, the music itself, and the emotion the music evokes.

Video disk sleeve for jazz drummer Tony Williams.

GÉLINÀS

"I listen to the music and talk with the performer when I can," she says. An album cover for Cher, for example, combined a conversation with the artist and Cher's interest in mysticism and tarot with artwork appealing to the majority of Cher's fans — young adult males. The indisputably memorable result is darkly detailed — even haunting.

Chase asserts that her best work happens when she doesn't think about it too hard. When something feels right to her, it usually is. "I believe if the designer doesn't feel it, the design won't communicate it." How does she develop such an innate sense of intuition? "The way I'd recommend is to try to find your own point of view, your own vision and style. Be prepared to work hard and don't be afraid to ask questions." It may help to have a supply of vitamins. "I spend a lot of energy just looking at things."

MARGO CHASE

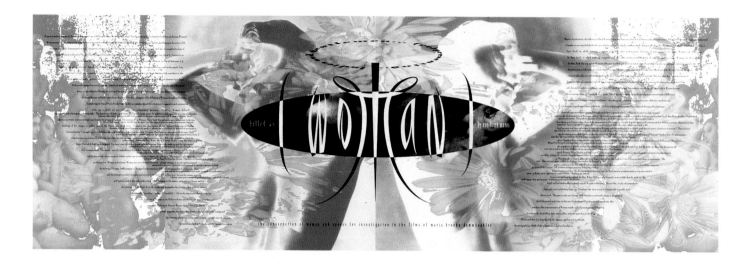

Layout for article on experimental typography and design.

Chase, whose first job in 1981 was designing plain wrap for a grocery store chain, claims she's motivated by a combination of fear and insecurity. "I'm always afraid I won't be able to solve the next problem as well as I did the last one. I need to keep proving I can." A college degree in biology and master's work in medical illustration were part of the varied background of education and interests that continue to personalize her graphics.

Packaging for Santa Cruz blue corn tortilla chips.

Logo for Madonna's "Like a Prayer" album.

Logo for "The Voices," a hard rock band.

"My design style is a result of combining the unrelated things that I like for visual and conceptual reasons. It's very layered and textural," she explains. "My work often communicates a feeling rather than a specific thought." Chase even creates her own letterforms.

MARGO CHASE

CD packaging for Cher's "Love Hurts" album.

She cites her design training as one of the most important parts of her career growth. "It introduced me to the ideas and ideals of design. I learn new techniques as I go along, but I always fall back on the traditional principles that I learned in school." She is not intimidated by the wave of technology that threatens to forever change the way design is produced. "Technology only changes the tools we use," she says, "not the way we think. The computer is a wonderful, powerful tool and I love the control it offers, but it doesn't solve design problems for me. I still have to design the same way I did before."

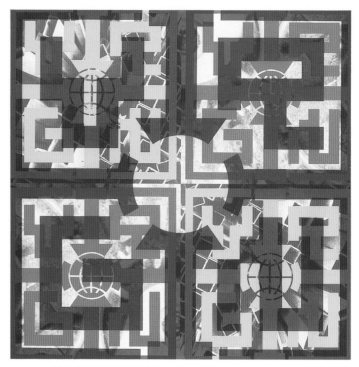

Generic sleeve for Virgin Records.

Stationery for Margo Chase Design.

*"This Could Be Such a
Beautiful World," promotional T-shirt design.*

In a thoughtful moment, Chase muses about her album design specialization: "This is a young business." She must pay constant attention to cultural fads, to clubs, to fashion. Her work, which has been called innovative, eclectic and mysterious, continues to evolve through her ability to be one step ahead of the trends, and to express herself to her audience clearly. "I like to talk. I think I'm articulate about design, conceptually as well as theoretically." Chase believes that taking calculated risks is the only way to create something new.

MARGO CHASE

Promotional poster, entitled "Germs," for Chase's speaking engagement.

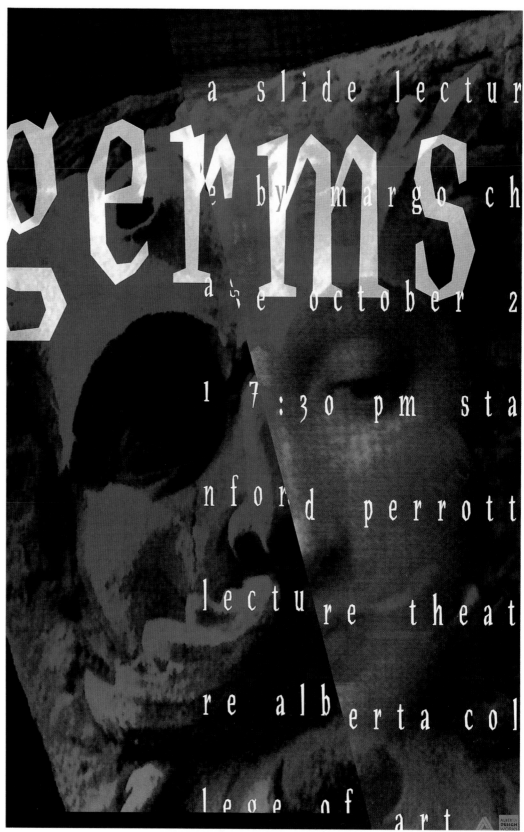

Her huge library is a great inspiration, as are the photographs she takes when traveling and her interest in medieval art and iconography. She collects old books from swap meets. She has a hefty portfolio of 35 mm slides that she takes with her on speaking engagements. Audiences seem particularly intrigued by her slide shows depicting the many stages that her work undergoes on the way to the final solution.

"Renaissance" album packaging.

Comprehensive for Virgin Records' generic sleeve.

Eschewing most big-budget accounts, Chase's business efforts are starting to become more product-oriented. "I'd like to design a product that generates a profit for me while I'm doing something else," she says. One successful attempt resulted in a line of coffee mugs called ViceVersa, which — in Chase's characteristic style — visually depicts opposite elements, such as fire and water, on either side of the mug. They have been sold nationally and featured by some museum shops in New York City.

SHEILA LEVRANT DE BRETTEVILLE

The Sheila Studio
New Haven, Connecticut, USA

Sheila Levrant de Bretteville is both teacher and creator. She teaches tolerance. "In order for society not to keep hurting ourselves, we must accept people without understanding them," she maintains. And she creates inspiration — "I dream of making myself and others into heroines and heroes."

Book cover and interior spread of The Motown Album.

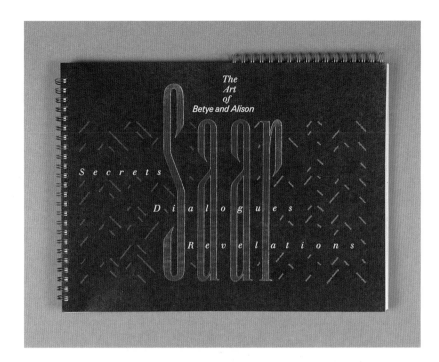

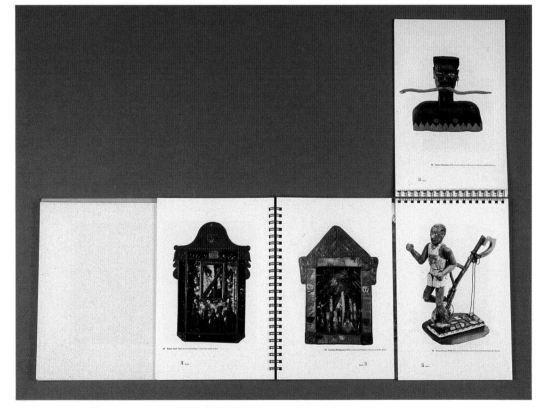

Catalog cover and interior spread for an exhibition of
"The Art of Betye and Alison Saar."

In 1990, de Bretteville designed one of her more well-known public artworks to honor Biddy Mason, a former slave and midwife. A year later, she was tasked to do a public art project in Los Angeles' Little Tokyo historic district. "These types of projects are rare, wonderful events that carry all my values," she explains. "In graphic design, I focus on ways to deeply involve a participating public — to create a structure to hold many voices. My favorite part is when I see an opportunity to do something that needs doing — some way to give the project an aura of imaginative truth, to embed it in a structure that allows us to hear from those from whom we have not yet heard."

SHEILA LEVRANT DE BRETTEVILLE

She founded the first women's design program at the California Institute for the Arts in 1971. Ten years later, she founded and chaired the department of Communication Design at Otis/Parsons, a division of the New School of Social Research. In 1990, de Bretteville accepted the position of professor and director of studies in graphic design at Yale University, the first tenured woman faculty member since the School of Art opened in 1865.

"I look for opportunity in a project; you have to have your opportunity lying in wait," de Bretteville asserts. "I believe in enlarging the problem of the client to include other values. In my compassion for others in the world, I demand a great deal. You must bring thinking to an operation, and ensure that the thinking and the design dovetail — what you communicate with what you make. I look for jobs that allow me to think through the problem, not simply package and decorate it. I really enjoy entertaining ideas that threaten what I have

Five different views of an 8' x 82' mural depicting life and contributions of Biddy Mason, midwife and former slave.

1850

She wins freedom in court.

She walks to California behind a wagon train.

She owns land.

previously thought," she says. de Bretteville became involved with women's causes in the early 1970s. But her work speaks to both sexes. She is quick to advise anyone who wonders about graphic arts as a career. "Re-read *The Wizard of Oz*," she suggests. "There is no need to sanctify famed persons. You have the heart, brains and courage to do what is needed."

SHEILA LEVRANT DE BRETTEVILLE

Poster for the "Architecture and Design Film Festival."

"I made the choice to enter the industry when I was still a teenager. Graphic design appeared to combine public and private needs, and seemed connected to a public in a more direct and interactive way than did artmaking. I think that I have created the kind of balance I need in my creative life. I sometimes think I would have liked to have sustained myself without any full-time jobs, never freelancing work with which I wasn't deeply connected. But I needed to support myself and was not convinced I could live off only the kinds of projects that I love most, and the time necessary for the completeness with which I do them."

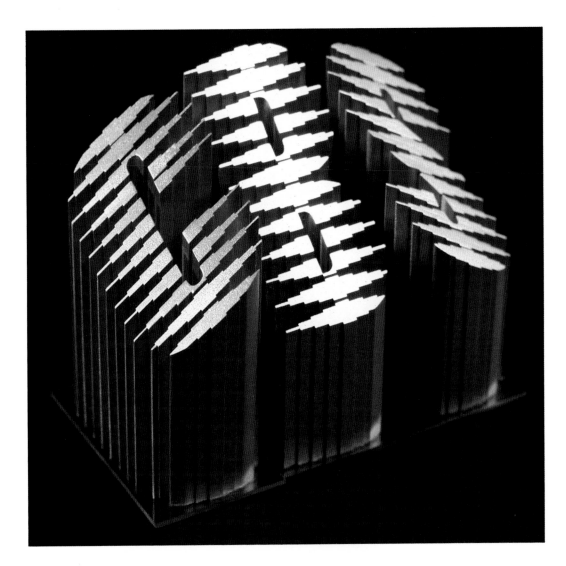

"Formal education," believes de Bretteville, "can be essential to imbuing the work with a depth of meaning and a symbolic content that can truly sustain the creator and the other participants in the work. It can enrich those who see, read, touch and, in whatever way, use what you do."

"In designing community graphics, I can't always wait for the client to come to me. I ask myself, who needs to know what this organization is offering that isn't getting the message? Then I use graphics to bridge that gap. I'm more interested in reaching the public who isn't being served. I think there is more need of that than in print graphics." For example, working with New Haven, Connecticut organizations, de Bretteville and her students researched, funded and produced billboards and other print graphics that offered information to the public who might seek help concerning hate crimes, domestic violence and women's reproductive rights.

Logo sculpture for CBS Cable, a short-lived fine arts channel.

31

SHEILA LEVRANT DE BRETTEVILLE

de Bretteville supports design organizations, although "we have to be clear whose needs are being served. Competitions support the organizations as much as they enhance the egos of the designers. Professional associations are good for the visibility and prestige of an industry, and can provide collective benefits for those in the profession in the same way that unions have argued on behalf of workers. To offer balance, there must be valued participation of those with alternative views of what graphic design is and might be. Organizations and conferences also provide a place for designers to be with others — a remnant of the public life diminished in our cities in the last decade."

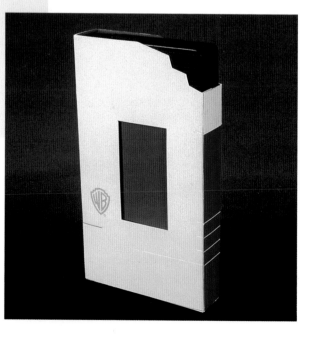

Letterhead, pouch box, and video box for Warner Bros. Records.

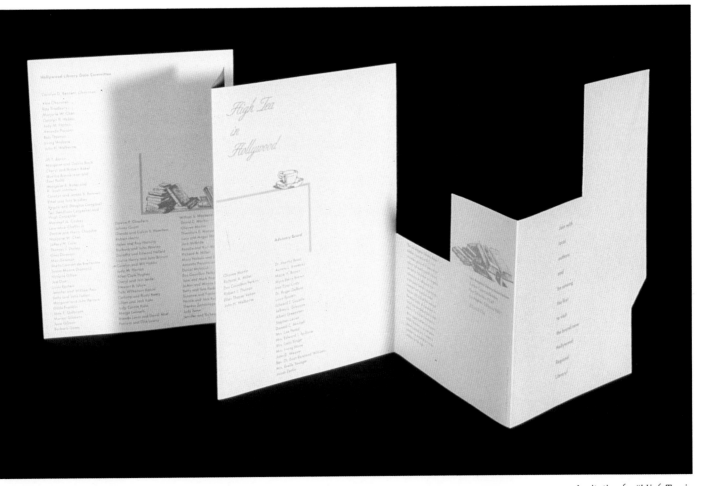

Invitation for "High Tea in Hollywood," the opening of a new public library designed by Frank Gehry.

Betye Saar, art catalog.

ANNA EYMONT

Eymont Kin Yee Hulett
Paddington, New South Wales, Australia

"I strongly believe in the latent possibilities in all of us," says Anna Eymont, who has been described as a relaxed, resourceful and self-motivated businesswoman unafraid of a challenge. "I love my work. But my one fear is running out of steam someday. Graphic art can be very difficult. I would advise new graphic designers to be prepared to work twice as hard as you think you need to." We also discovered that she doesn't take herself too seriously. "The easiest thing about being a designer," she says, "is cleaning your desk before starting a project."

"Water," a presentation folder on wastewater reuse.

Logo, menus, and stationery for Bobbin Inn.

Community education logo
for the Waterboard of
New South Wales.

Eymont knows something about hard work and difficult choices. She left her native Poland surreptitiously in the late 1970s to join her father and brother in Australia. Though she struggled with the English language and foreign culture, she managed to overcome the obstacles through persistence. She quickly rose to the top of the design field and operated her own studio, Eymont Design, before joining Myriam Kin-Yee (and, later, Alison Hulett) to establish EKH Design.

ANNA EYMONT

These days, she frequently returns to a more liberated Poland to lecture and investigate the possibility of someday setting up a branch studio there. "There are talented artists in Poland, who are very supportive," Eymont notes. She has also explored the possibility of a satellite office in Southeast Asia.

It was by accident that she found out she could make a living at commercial art. At first, she had chosen to become a painter. "Design work," Eymont contends, "is very methodical. But painting is loose and expressive." She enjoyed the association with creative, intellectual people. Poland has a high regard for their artists; visitors claim every third shop on the main streets is an art gallery. It was in this atmosphere that Eymont's talent was cultivated. "My primary motivation then and now was the need to prove to my family that I could succeed in business as a migrant. I needed to prove myself outside my own country."

Posters for the National Australian Maritime Museum.

HUMAN RIGHTS AND EQUAL OPPORTUNITY COMMISSION

1990

Brochure for the Australian Human Rights and Equal Opportunity Commission.

"Myriam Kin-Yee and I set up EKH Design so that it is very democratic," says Eymont. "We decided early on that we would not be controlled by the business — instead, we would control it. So we arranged for four weeks' holiday the first year of business, and increased that the second year. And we knew that if one of us went away for awhile to take a course or travel, the business would not suffer: the other partner would ensure the work was produced on time and at the same level of quality." It's a question of priorities, says Eymont. "We all love our work, but we want to make sure it doesn't get the best of us."

ANNA EYMONT

Promotional material for Lincoln Downs, a country resort.

It is Eymont, a graduate of the Warsaw Academy of Fine Arts and lecturer at renowned Australian colleges, who has the best business sense of the trio. But clients inevitably choose to work with EKH because Eymont and her partners strive to make them comfortable. "Of course, they expect great design. But we truly do have their best interest at heart," Eymont asserts. "And we also want to save them money. We're competent, talented designers who are highly service-oriented." And they have the teamwork aspect down to an art. Eymont says, "We put all the egos on the back burner and look at the problem critically. There are times when one of us does the layout, another determines the colors, and a third finishes the typography."

Presentation folder and brochure for GHD International.

EKH Design works because the three are very different. Eymont is organized, efficient and analytical. Kin-Yee calls herself colorful and spontaneous. Hulett is worldly and sophisticated. "Each personality appeals to different clients," says Eymont. "We complement each other." "The work is done with three bodies and one head," says Kin-Yee. "We are continually influenced by all the people who work with us."

BROADER HORIZONS FOR WOMEN AT WORK

The Affirmative Action Agency
1st Floor 65 Berry St
North Sydney NSW 2060
Telephone: (02) 963 4999

Design and Production: Eymont Kin-Yee Design Pty Ltd

Poster and brochures for the Affirmative Action Agency.

AFFIRMATIVE ACTION AGENCY

AFFIRMATIVE ACTION FOR WOMEN:
GUIDELINES FOR IMPLEMENTA'
IN THE PRIVATE SECTOR

AFFIRMATIVE ACTION

ANNA EYMONT

Annual report for OPSM Industries Limited.

But Eymont is not all serious business and organization. "She's a good skier, a great tennis player," confides Hulett, "and she loves cappuccino." Eymont admits to a great love of "the finer things in life" — "good music, good food." It comes across in her design work: "I think it makes my craft a bit more refined."

"Movies at the Metcalfe" poster for the State Library of New South Wales.

Menus for Bayswater Brasserie.

The three partners, who have all traveled extensively and lived abroad, represent a wide international exposure. Explains Eymont, "We took the best of Australia, with its sunshine and holidays, and combined that with American and European work ethics and came up with our business style. The most important things are that we enjoy working and that we are serving our customers well." And, because workdays that end at 4 a.m. are not uncommon, she adds, "We're very lucky that we can laugh when things become difficult. If you can't laugh, there's no sense doing it." The group has a way of making even a simple interview into an enjoyable occasion. Says Kin-Yee, "We may not be millionaires, but we're very happy."

Logo and bottle label for Australian Spring Water.

APRIL GREIMAN

April Greiman, Inc.
Los Angeles, California, USA

When we asked April Greiman the name of her favorite book, we didn't expect to hear Art and Technology Meet Spirituality in a Changing Economy. She patiently explained her choice of subject. "Over the past few years, I've been influenced by physicists," she said. "I've read a lot of mythology and physics. I'm trying to find systems of order that inspire things to happen in the universe. These studies are not so much directly influential into form as they are into my idea of the evolution of consciousness, and, therefore, communication."

Cover of Hybrid Imagery: The Fusion of Technology and Graphic Design, *book featuring work of April Greiman, Inc.*

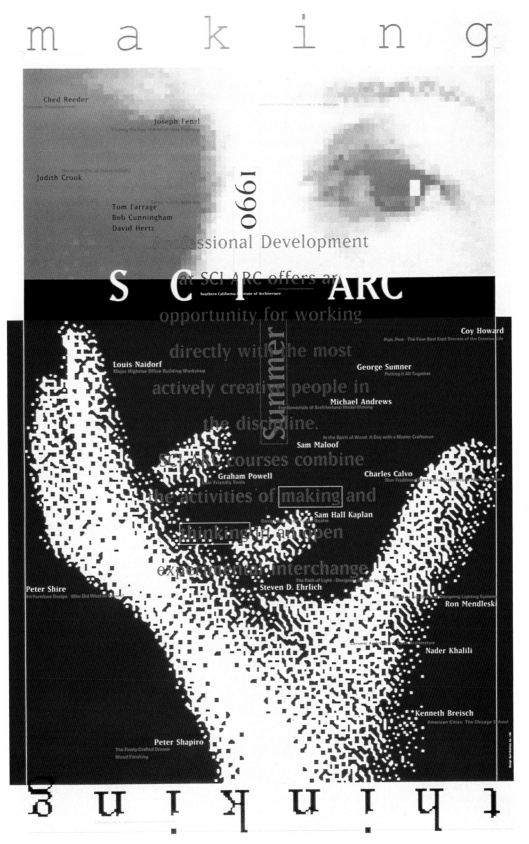

Poster for *Southern California Institute of Architecture.*

Greiman's recreational interest in physics is part of a philosophy that steps far out of the circle of conservative approaches less successful designers favor. "My work operates at the intersection of the appropriate and the unexpected," she says. "The process is the most stimulating and significant idea motivating the work." Her work is a synthesis of photography, collaging, video and writing, as well as a phenomenal amount of study and concentration. "This is not a job for me — it is who I am."

As one of the most well-known pioneers of computer graphics, Greiman insists many designers haven't yet scratched the surface of what computers can do. "Traditional hand skills and training combined with cutting-edge software yields solutions integrating a classic sense of form with an unconventional approach. Our design solutions are both practical and memorable." Greiman's studio had a big head-start on technology. They bought their first computer in 1984 — "they all made fun of us" — and now own five. "Much of computer design is similar, but there's a layer of surprise that occurs that wouldn't if you were using traditional methods. New tools mean new tasks, and, thus, new content. Emerging global networks exalt the smallest coherent system — the individual mind and spirit."

APRIL GREIMAN

> ogether effectively, the building will
>
> rstand the problems of our collaborators
>
> understand ours, engineering is or
>
> challenging activity. And when it is
>
> or even better, great architecture, it
>
> warding."
>
> llege of Art, London, on December 17, 1987 in association with the College's

Summer program book for Southern California Institute of Architecture.

She designs through "a collective effort. I can get lost for endless hours when working on a painting. Everyone in the studio gets involved in the research." She employs three designers, two interns and one freelance graphic artist for special projects. "We have a playful environment, but we're relentless perfectionists with high standards. Novice designers may not understand that the way we work is not the way most studios approach design. I make sure they're all pushed out of the nest at some point before they decide to settle here."

Invitational poster for Sir Jack Zunz.

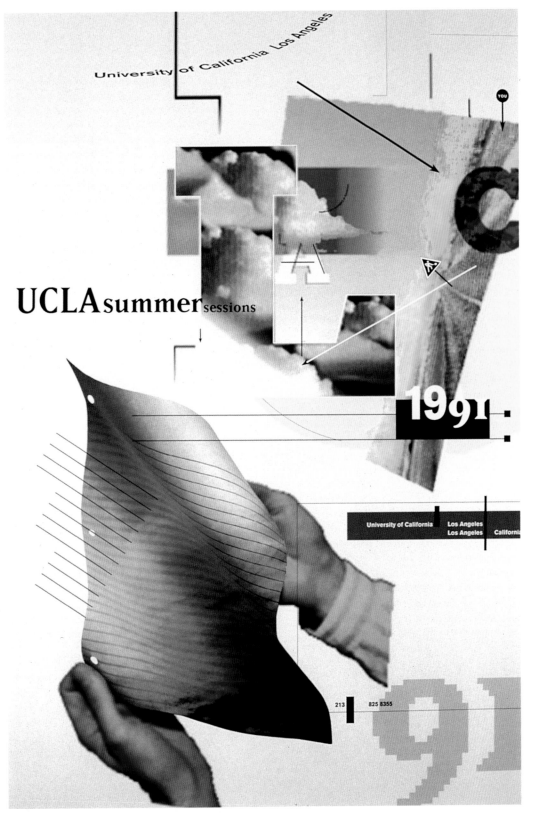

Poster for summer sessions of the University of California at Los Angeles.

The environment at Greiman's studio, like most of what she does, is innovative. She organized the week so that Fridays are working sessions. "It gives everyone a day in the studio to themselves, when we don't work with the public and use the answering service." She says, "We all eat lunch together. And we have music playing all day long. All kinds of music. Jazz, industrial, rap, Nat King Cole, Annie Lennox, opera. We had k.d. Lange on most of last week."

APRIL GREIMAN

Woven textile for "Harlequin."

Stationery for Cerritos Center for the Performing Arts.

Greiman moved to California from her native New York in 1976 when she was offered an identity project for a Beverly Hills company. She stayed because of the desert and the natural environment, and founded her business in 1978. She was not the first in her family to explore graphic design. Her grandmother was a scholarship art student. "But my dad and brother are scientists," she says. Maybe that's where she got her interest in physics.

Tile motifs for Cerritos Center for the Performing Arts.

"Vitra Neocon," a fold-out poster for Vitra Seating, Inc., chair manufacturer.

How did she achieve her success? "Beats me!" she'll say, and amend that: "Timing, and a good adventurous spirit." She didn't agonize over career choices when she was young. "I've never been highly practical," she'll tell you, and laugh. Greiman gives a lot of credit for her success to her clients. "They're the best. They never ask us to change things because they understand what we do: they're highly evolved."

APRIL GREIMAN

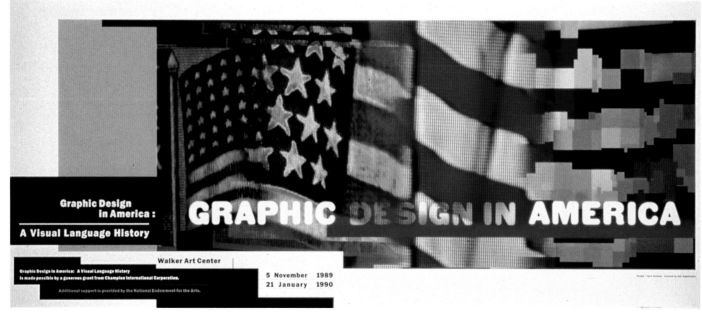

Poster and billboard for "Graphic Design in America," an exhibit of the Walker Art Center.

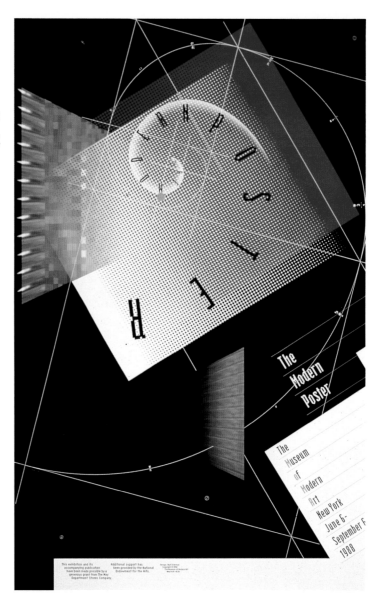

Poster for the Museum of Modern Art's exhibit, "The Modern Poster."

She copes with stress by "meditating and treating my physical self generously, because I get a lot more done when I'm rested and relaxed. I'll switch hours or sleep longer when I need to," says Greiman, who once shared her home with 10 pet cats. "I'm simply honest with my clients and myself."

*Stationery system for
Roto NDI Architects.*

Restaurant signage for China Club.

She's working on her second book, "which will concentrate more on the meaning of the work and the philosophy behind it." After it's published? "I'd like to take a year off and paint with the computer; do giant pastel drawings. But right now, my work is so fulfilling, I don't think about what comes next."

CATHERINE HAUGHTON

*Haughton Brazeau Design
Toronto, Ontario, Canada*

"Everyone in the studio has something to contribute when we're looking for design ideas," says Catherine Haughton, one half of the Toronto-based graphics team Haughton Brazeau. "Even our receptionist is encouraged to offer an opinion, because she looks at things from a different perspective."

*Newsletter for a Ford of
Canada car dealer.*

Circus characters featured on stationery for Haughton Brazeau.

After a few minutes with Haughton, one would expect she'd support a democratic environment. Not only is she easy to talk to, she listens carefully and her replies indicate she values other opinions. Her studio numbers eight members, including herself and her husband/ partner Philip Brazeau. "I wouldn't want it to be much bigger," she confides. "Each designer brings different talents and skills to a project. Our works don't carry a specific look. That's done intentionally. I feel we should not rely on a style to which we've grown accustomed. If I can identify a work from a style, I view it as a failure."

Promotional items for the "Second Annual Haughton Brazeau Air Show & Family Picnic," a thank-you for clients, staff, and suppliers.

CATHERINE HAUGHTON

Haughton Brazeau opened its doors almost a decade ago with virtually no money and no clients. But Haughton believed there was only so far one could go working for someone else. "It took persistence and a lot of reliance on each other," she says. The two designers had a great deal going for them, including Haughton's skills as a visual choreographer and interpreter. And her optimism may have been a factor — she never considered the possibility that they would not succeed.

Graphics run in Haughton's family, with a history that harkens back over 35 years. "My family provided some good teaching and advice," she says. "I also made a lot of mistakes in our business, and learned from them."

Self-promotion, entitled "Winning Combinations."

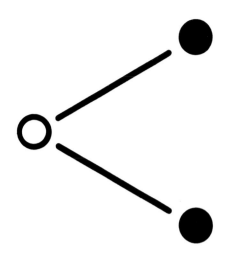

Unifying symbol for NewTel Enterprises Ltd.

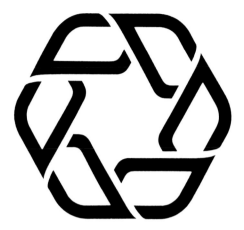

Identity for Anderson Public Relations.

Annual report for NewTel Enterprises Ltd.

Haughton is one of a rare breed of designers who can also illustrate, although that skill is not easily applied to the commercial work that currently comprises most of their jobs. "Painting scenes and still-lifes is very pleasurable for me. Years ago, I also did portraiture for a while."

Haughton likes to keep busy, and her schedule proves it. "There are always the trade shows like AIGA, and I'm involved in public speaking at the college level. I enjoy conferences and contests, because we all need a little idealism to get us going. After attending meetings, there's always a lot of adrenaline pumping. I am also involved in business associations and organizations, so I learn about the issues that are important to our customers."

CATHERINE HAUGHTON

*Stationery for photographer
Barbara Cole.*

BaRbARa CoLE

BaRbARa CoLE

BarbAra CoLE
pHoTogRAphy

176 joHN StrEET,
suiTe 4#4,
ToroNTo Ontario, Canada
M5T 1x5
telEphone
And FacsiMile
416 599 5822

176 joHN StrEET,
suiTe 4#4,
ToroNTo Ontario, Canada
M5T 1x5

telEphone
And FacsiMile

416 599 5822

"I admire designers who design cutlery and plates and other objects, and I hope to try that someday," Haughton says. "I'd also like to apply my skills to producing corporate videos." But today, she is challenged by working with customers, asking questions and brainstorming, although — "I'd rather leave the production aspect to someone else."

Annual report for Household Finance Corporation.

Ontario Hydro's diverse market is depicted in its annual report.

Annual report for Markborough Properties.

"There is a sense of conservatism in Canada that's slowly changing, but sometimes this attitude can still hold us back," Haughton says. "Many clients are afraid to take chances, and that's difficult for us because we're motivated by doing things exciting and dynamic. But, as our clients become more educated about the value of graphics, we are gradually seeing a revolution. Customers are more prepared to become creatively involved."

CATHERINE HAUGHTON

When Haughton Brazeau was launched, the computer was just emerging as a product with graphic applications. "It allowed us to streamline our design, and make our work much more efficient and profitable. Today, we don't use the computer as a creative tool, but as a production tool to develop jobs faster and with better control. Non-designers mistakenly think the computer is a panacea for all problems, but it can't think for you." It took her studio six years to learn how to use computers productively, because they were all schooled in traditional design methods. "It's not as easy as taking a few night courses and reading a manual."

Annual report for
World Wildlife Fund Canada.

Corporate brochure for Wood Gundy, international investors.

At home, Haughton is renowned for her outstanding desserts. "My personal time is precious," she asserts, "and I treasure the solitude. But I also enjoy creating rich and unusual dishes that other people love to eat." Her next challenge? Raising daughter Jessy Quinn, born in the summer of 1992. "She's changed my outlook on a lot of things." Haughton wasted no time getting her daughter acquainted with the graphics environment: Jessy Quinn was only weeks old when she made her first visit to the studio.

JANE HOPE

Taxi Design
Montreal, Quebec, Canada

"**I**'m motivated by brains and beauty," says Jane Hope, "although beauty doesn't carry any quantifiable value in our culture. The art world has lately become loaded with extraneous meaning. It is moving away from producing things that are simply a pleasure to look at. That was one reason I went into advertising — I believed that I could create things that had value and touched people on a grand scale."

Bar coaster for Smirnoff Vodka,
"Rouge comme l'enfer" (*Red hot*).

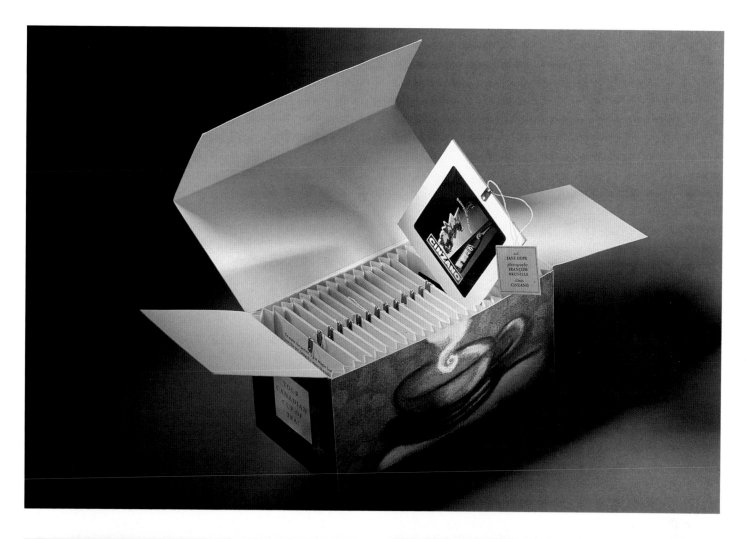

Promotional packaging for Maple Leaf Tea.

JANE HOPE

She is discouraged by the growing number of graphic artists who design primarily to jolt their audiences. "Elegance is a combination of intelligence and beauty. When I design, I try to inject that quality into my work. I want things to be pertinent and remarkable, built around the central core of an idea."

Hope attributes the majority of her success to her ability to locate the right mix of people to accomplish a task. "Some of it is luck," she admits, "but the rest of it is skill in choosing the right person and putting him or her in a position to shine." She believes in giving people "enough room to work." "I'm fortunate in that I know so many talented people, and the group of us have been able to accomplish some wonderful things."

Poster for "L'art dans la rue" (Art in the Street), *a City of Montreal event.*

L'ART DANS LA RUE

VIVRE
MONTRÉAL

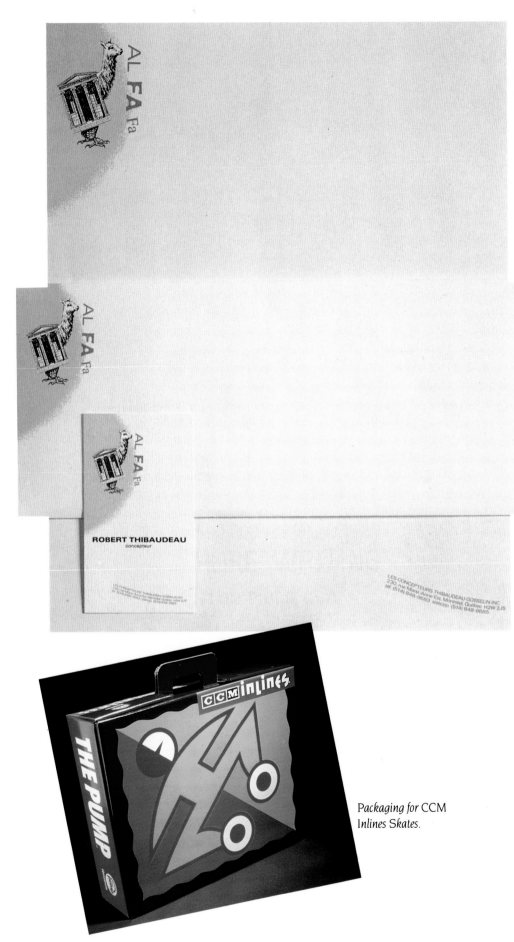

Stationery for Alfafa,
advertising agency.

ROBERT THIBAUDEAU
concepteur

Packaging for CCM
Inlines Skates.

"My definition of career success is the feeling you get when you're present among those for whom you have great respect. For example, when you go to Italy, and you see magnificent paintings and sculpture — beauty that gives you such a thrill and inspires you. These things make you strive to be part of such greatness." Hope knows something about success: she was nominated by the Toronto advertising newspaper, *Strategy*, as one of Quebec's five best advertising art directors in 1990, and one of the 10 best in Canada by *Creative Source* in 1992.

For a designer who gets easily carried away with projects ("I love the smell of printed proofs"), the most difficult thing about her work is avoiding getting too personally involved with each task. "The creative process is so much an extension of oneself, that when you experience the inevitable period where things aren't quite working on paper for a project, it's frustrating — you start questioning your very existence!"

JANE HOPE

Poster and postcard for architectural conference, "Montreal 1990."

The first step in creating a piece from concept to conclusion is to find the idea, says Hope. "But it's the design process that puts an idea in its best light. It makes it digestible. It's the jam you put on the pill to make it easier to swallow." Hope, who received her schooling at the Ontario College of Art and the Université Concordia in Montreal, also believes education is a vital component in the process. "Creativity," she maintains, "is fueled by knowledge. You need as many reference points as you can get. Graduate work is probably only necessary for teachers. But some sort of undergraduate work is helpful when refining the craft, which is the most important part of design." Even awards have a function in a designer's creative lifestyle. "Awards remind us that we're not crazy to be up at 3 a.m., fussing with details."

Billboards for McDonald's, "Je ne peux pas y résister" (I can't resist).

JANE HOPE

After a conversation with Hope, it's not hard to start believing in the singular power of beautiful visuals. Her enthusiasm is contagious, and she applies it to her belief in the good of society, as well as her expectations of her own future. She will tell you that certain personality traits, especially energy and confidence, are important attributes to her work. But she cites other characteristics as well. It always helps, she claims, to be charming, friendly, firm and aggressive — and to love your work.

Hope chose the design field by accident. She studied fine arts — history and art classes were her favorites — but ended up in advertising, which she calls a "very aggressive" environment. But it, surprisingly, suited her well for several years. In 1992, Hope cofounded Taxi Design, a studio whose philosophy is to "doubt the traditional — create the exceptional." After that? "I'll get into 3-D things," including designing furnishings for the home, objects, dishes, fabrics. "Products are design people can buy."

Campaign logo for Tireurs d'élite (Sharpshooters), media service professionals.

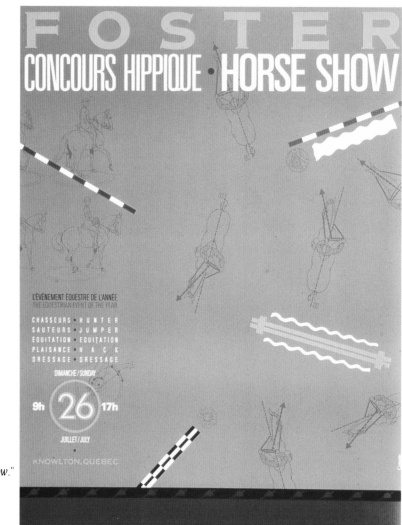

Poster for "Foster Horse Show."

Stationery for Lynn Paradis, psychologist.

Poster for Biodôme, the living museum.

DITI KATONA

Concrete Design Communications
Toronto, Ontario, Canada

The first time we spoke with Diti Katona, we complimented her on her name. It was so lyrical and unusual, we said, it sounded like the moniker for a famous actress or singer. She laughed. "Or a stripper!" she said.

Katona's sense of humor not only animates an interview, but it also has become an important part of her design. Combine that with a desire to enliven the graphic look of corporate Toronto, and Katona can boast a personal formula for success. "It seemed much of the design and logos I saw in business were slick and without content — simply

"Printed in Canada" brochure and press kit for the Canadian Printing Industries Association.

gray." She and partner/
husband John Pylypczak
believed that conservative
design could have a vitality to
it and still be corporate-savvy.
They weren't alone in this
belief, and, for the first few
years after Concrete Design
Communications was
founded, they never had to
solicit work. "We didn't even
have a brochure."

Stationery for Concrete Design Communications Inc.

Moving announcement
for Concrete Design.

What are the *three* most important
elements to the
survival of any business today?

L O C A T I O N !
L O C A T I O N !
L O C A T I O N !

*Well – not having ever heeded conventional
wisdom before, we're bucking the trend and
moving west! So, as of May 4, 1992, you will
find us in our
new (and freshly
painted!) offices at
2 Silver Avenue.*

DITI KATONA

Brochure introducing Zapata's line of spring 1993 clothing.

"We started our business because there was really nowhere else for me to work," says Katona, who at that time had already been affiliated with what she considered the best design firms in the area. Now Concrete Design has seven full-time staffers and may eventually double that number, but they have no interest in becoming any larger than that. "I'd like to stay in touch with all aspects of design," Katona explains. "I think the size of a company makes a difference in your commitments and priorities. If we were too large, I think the quality would diminish."

Brochure introducing Zapata's line of spring 1993 clothing.

Cover and inside spread of an employee annual report.

Success for Katona, who has been featured in magazines such as *Communication Arts, Studio* and *One on One*, will "never" be defined as money or fame. "It's earning the respect of my peers and clients. I'm honored when they listen and when I can motivate them with my ideas and experience."

"Someday, I'd like to work with professionals from other disciplines and create something really tremendous," Katona says. Those professionals might range from architects and industrial designers to photographers and engineers. And the product? "A car, or a fountain, or something three-dimensional and appealing to the mass-market. I work so much in print that I begin to wonder what else I could try. When everyone's equally creative and talented, projects can have great results." One of her favorites was a series of brochures for a young Canadian fashion designer. They shipped his clothing line to a photographer in Los Angeles, so that the fashions could be photographed with a desert backdrop. Notes Katona, "I love to work in fashion, because they let me do whatever I want!"

DITI KATONA

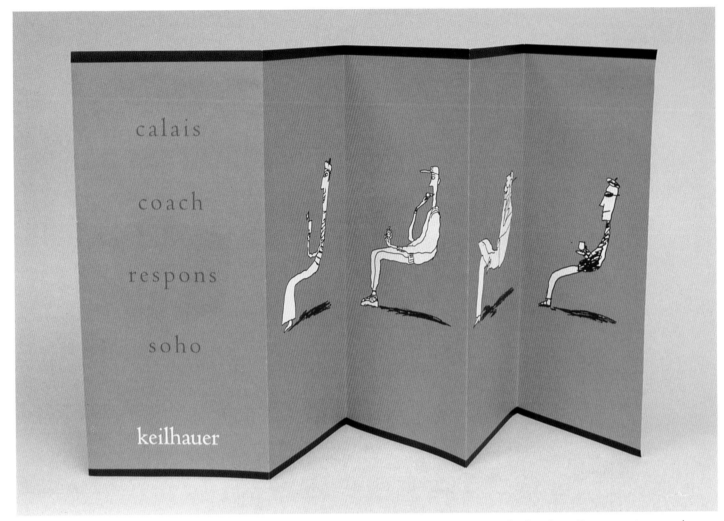

New products brochure for Keilhauer, a seating manufacturer.

Katona visits Hungary almost every summer to work with friends there who make their living as designers and artists. "My parents emigrated from Hungary in 1956," she says, "and I think the cultural difference gives my work a special perspective." That perspective is always filtered through a bright and optimistic look on life. She calls her family "the luckiest people in the world." "Canada is a beautiful place to live. We've never been through a war, we're not cold, not hungry." And, needless to say, her work adds to her contentment.

Employee annual report for Noranda Inc., a natural resource company.

Stationery for DuVerre,
a housewares retailer.

*Self-promotional calendar
for Concrete Design.*

A career in commercial art was far from her thoughts when, in college, she became involved in a welcoming committee for a conference of the American Institute of Graphic Artists. It was there she met many industry greats, like Kit Hinrichs and Woody Pirtle. "I was majoring in fine arts," she said, but soon changed her concentration to design in typography. "I remember thinking, 'what a neat thing to do for a living.'"

DITI KATONA

"I still love pop art, like Andy Warhol. And I'll always enjoy etching, drawing, painting, silk-screening and film. I love to set my own type, and to try making things by hand." Those may be her favorite aesthetic pursuits, but Katona's talents are not limited to art. She also is very good at: "Going on vacation, figure skating, eating food and watching television." Explains Katona, "I love to watch news from the States because Canadian news is so boring — nothing happens here. Television in the United States is so lively and entertaining — someday it may even give me some new ideas for my work!"

Panorama, *employee newsmagazine on the future of Canada.*

PANORAMA

A BIMONTHLY NEWSMAGAZINE FOR NORANDA GROUP EMPLOYEES • DECEMBER 1991   LA REVUE D'INFORMATION BIMESTRIELLE DES EMPLOYÉS DU GROUPE NORANDA • DÉCEMBRE 1991

CANADA ~ OUR FUTURE
Noranda Group employees speak out about Canada's constitutional debate

LE CANADA ~ NOTRE AVENIR
Les employés du groupe Noranda donnent leur avis sur le débat constitutionnel canadien

Annual report for Northern Telecom.

"Flexplan" benefits package for a natural resource company.

Annual report for First
Mercantile Currency Fund.

SIOBHAN KEANEY

Siobhan Keaney
London, England

"**F**rom day one, I did what I wanted to do in design," Siobhan Keaney laughs. "I'm totally spoiled."

Keaney has never had to market herself. Her style has become recognizable in England and parts of Europe. "For years, graphic design was confined to flat images. I attempt to take it further." Clients seek her out, based on her reputation. "When I complete a project, the response I prefer to get from my clients is, 'I wasn't expecting that.' I like to take them off into my own world. Freedom is the most important element to me in design. The more abstract, the better."

Poster for TDK videotapes.

*Promotional materials for
The Mill, a post-production company.*

On her own since 1985, Keaney is the embodiment of a non-conformist. "I worked for three London design groups, then it was a natural progression to my own studio." She portrays herself through her work. "A little more money would be good," she jokes, "but primarily, I have to enjoy the work and I must get on well with the client to consider the job." She has turned down lucrative projects, and, in fact, eschews larger clients. "When big budgets are involved, so much money is at stake that people will pull back and restrain you. I want a project I'll love and be proud of."

SIOBHAN KEANEY

Her style is active, with a lot of movement apparent in the composition. "I don't tailor my work for specific projects," she says. "I am 'anti-grids.' I couldn't work from a constructed brief. I may have a selfish way of going about it, but I need this kind of freedom to produce my kind of work." And her approach has been more than successful. "If you enjoy what you do, it has to come through, and I love this. It's not a nine-to-five job, it's a way of life. Sometimes it does interfere with a social life. But in the studio, time has no meaning."

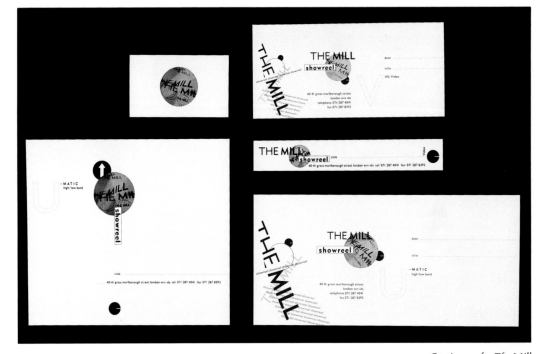

Stationery for The Mill.

"Freedom" stamp for an exhibition at The Design Museum in London.

Subscription promotion for EYE Magazine.

Keaney graduated from the London College of Printing in 1982 and started work in the middle of a design boom in London. "Some of the worst design ever was produced in England in the 1980s," Keaney maintains. "It was the style that was so poor — pastel colors developed to look good without content, rationale or appropriateness. Clients were encouraged to spend freely for unprofessional design and the British government backed the designers. That decade left a bad taste for a lot of clients, and left a legacy of horrible design for the industry."

Poster for Seymour Powell, a product design company.

SIOBHAN KEANEY

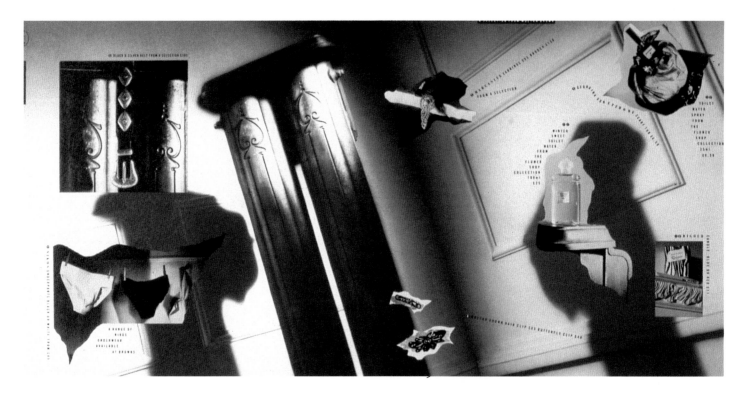

Keaney hand-renders all her type, as she learned in school. She regrets that many students today do not know how to do the same. "With serifs, I have to be careful; if I play with them, they can get crude. You must treat them with sensitivity, rather than twisting them and throwing them around. That's why education is important — it gives you a base of rules. Without them, you're floundering. When you understand the rules, then you break them." She makes her own rules. For example, instead of hiring models for one of her more well-known projects, she used friends. "And I have props I collect from hardware stores and sheds in boxes around the studio," Keaney says.

Christmas accessories brochure for Browns, a high-fashion retailer.

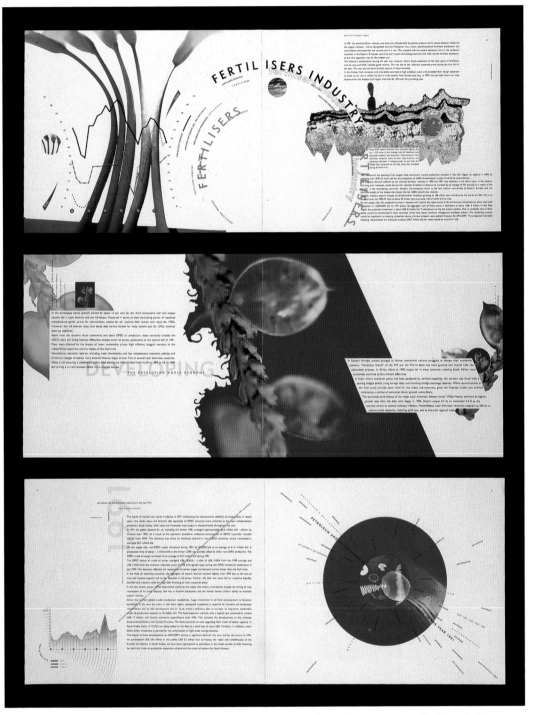

A Middle-East investment corporation is one of her best clients, and her work for them consistently wins awards in British competitions. A recent annual report she designed won numerous accolades. "Up until four years ago, they were producing the typical annual report. That changed because a designer said, 'you don't have to do it this way.'"

Annual report for Apicorp, emphasizing the importance of nature and its resources.

SIOBHAN KEANEY

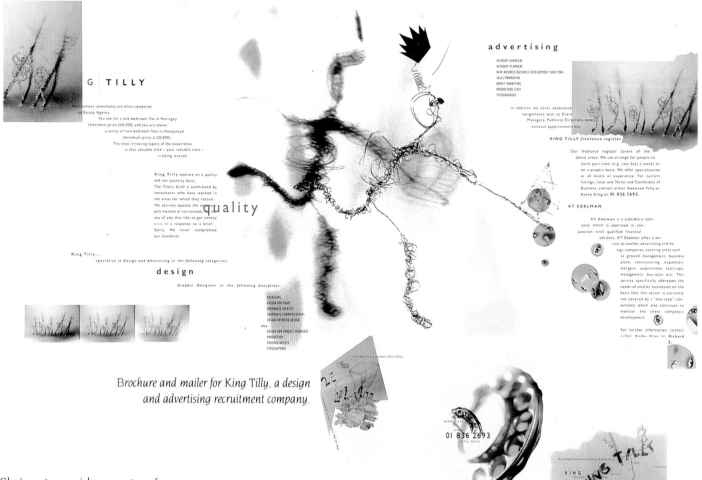

G | TILLY

Recruitment consultants are often compared
to Estate Agents.
You ask for a one bedroom flat in Haringey
(maximum price £60,000) and you are shown
a series of two bedroom flats in Hampstead
(minimum price £120,000).
The most irritating aspect of the experience
is that valuable time – your valuable time –
is being wasted.

King Tilly operate on a quality,
and not quantity basis.
The Client brief is assimilated by
consultants who have worked in
the areas for which they recruit.
We actively oppose the conveyor
belt method of recruitment. If
any of you that like to get twenty
c.v.s in a response to a brief...
Sorry. We never compromise
our standards.

quality

King Tilly...
specialize in Design and Advertising in the following categories;

design

Graphic Designers in the following disciplines;

PACKAGING
DESIGN FOR PRINT
CORPORATE IDENTITY
CORPORATE COMMUNICATIONS
3D AND INTERIOR DESIGN
also
DESIGN AND PROJECT MANAGERS
PRODUCTION
FINISHED ARTISTS
TYPOGRAPHERS

advertising

ACCOUNT HANDLERS
ACCOUNT PLANNERS
NEW BUSINESS/BUSINESS DEVELOPMENT DIRECTORS
SALES PROMOTION
DIRECT MARKETING
PRODUCTION STAFF
TYPOGRAPHERS

In addition we cover associated
assignments such as Event
Managers, Publicity Directors, international appointments etc.

KING TILLY freelance register

Our freelance register covers all the
above areas. We can arrange for people to
work part-time (e.g. two days a week) or
on a project basis. We offer specialisation
at all levels of experience. For current
listings, rates and Terms and Conditions of
Business, contact either Deborah Tilly or
Kathy King on 01 836 2693.

KT EDELMAN

KT Edelman is a subsidiary company which is operated in con-
junction with qualified financial
advisors. KT Edelman offer a service to smaller advertising and design companies, covering areas such
as growth management, business
plans, restructuring, expansion,
mergers, acquisitions, start-ups,
management buy-outs etc. This
service specifically addresses the
needs of smaller businesses on the
basis that this sector is currently
not covered by a "one-stop" con-
sultancy which also continues to
monitor the client company's
development.

For further information, contact
either Kathy King or Richard
J.

*Brochure and mailer for King Tilly, a design
and advertising recruitment company.*

She's not an avid supporter of new technology. "I like to touch paper and pen," Keaney explains, "not look at a computer screen. Everyone uses the same programs and you can recognize that in the design. Some software can be used to draw, but even then, you have to know what you want to do, otherwise you can sit for hours, just playing. Computers are fantastic when used well, but everyone's using them too much and it's becoming a big mess."

Typographic images for a Letraset catalog.

Brochure for Seymour Powell, commemorating the company's fifth year anniversary.

Stationery for Seymour Powell.

Keaney, accompanied by assistant Deborah Tilly, stopped by our studio in Washington, D.C. on a U.S.A. cross-country trip. "Travel is one of the best things you can do. It teaches tolerance and understanding of other people. Britain, after all, is an island, and if you don't go outside it, your beliefs can become insular," she contends. "Places like America change so much just between the states." Film buffs would be interested to know she called it her "Thelma & Louise" trip — "except we don't plan to end up in the Grand Canyon."

JUDY KIRPICH

Grafik Communications
Alexandria, Virginia, USA

"I designed a firm and a way of working," Judy Kirpich contends. "Grafik Communications is a collaboration. I hire the best talent I can find, and many of my staff can outdesign me. I don't consider myself a star in the design industry."

Kirpich's credentials indicate otherwise. Her numerous awards are from the best of the best, including The Type Directors Club, American Institute of Graphic Artists, the Art Directors Clubs of Washington and New York,

Introductory brochure for the National Museum of the American Indian.

Poster for "Systems Center 1989 User Conference."

and national, regional and local Addys from the American Advertising Association. She lectures frequently at the Smithsonian Institution and calls her style "old school," not flashy. "But my stuff is legible," she says.

She's not your average Washington worker, bucking the trends that advocate long hours, short vacations and a heavy dependence on day care services. "In business, you must first get your priorities straight. Do you want to make money? Be famous? Work and still have a home life? You can't have it all. You must decide how much you are willing to give up. Design awards have not changed my life at all. They are pieces of paper on the wall. What's important to me is to make sure I don't miss my two kids growing up."

JUDY KIRPICH

THE · WAVE · OF · THE · FUTURE

"Wave of the Future" poster for VM Software.

"My own priorities? Not to be rich. Not to be famous. Not to own my own business; I'm very content being a partner with Alex. I think it's the day-to-day things that matter. I want autonomy. What matters is that one of my staff who has a sick father can leave indefinitely and have a job when he comes back. That changes their lives, and changes mine, too. I believe in improving each other's lives in small, significant ways."

Direct-mail promotion for Virginia Lithograph.

VIRGINIA LITHOGRAPH

BEST IN SHOW

Promotional box for Esse brand recycled paper.

Kirpich started Grafik because she didn't want to work in high heels. "I design barefoot, in jeans." In conservative, high-powered Washington, she is a successful enigma. "I don't want the persona," she says. "I come from a socialist background. I explain to clients that they won't just work with me, they'll work with a team. We keep overtime to a minimum and pay designers for it. We educate clients on what it takes to do something and why; for example, why developing a logo won't be completed in a week."

With a B.A. in sociology and an M.A. in landscape architecture from Harvard University Graduate School of Design, Kirpich actually has no formal background in commercial art. "In landscape architecture, I learned about construction and materials. Then I discovered I liked type better than trees."

JUDY KIRPICH

KELLY   FEENEY

*Museum catalog showcasing drawings and
sketches of Josef Albers.*

In 1977, when there were only
about four major design firms
in Washington who all
produced Swiss-looking
design, Kirpich started her
career in the museum
industry. Her work was
unusual, and soon won
acclaim. "I thought the piece
should follow the marketing of
the client. I didn't think it
should all have one look. I
thought each piece should do
a specific job."

*"Information Age" poster
for the National Museum
of American History.*

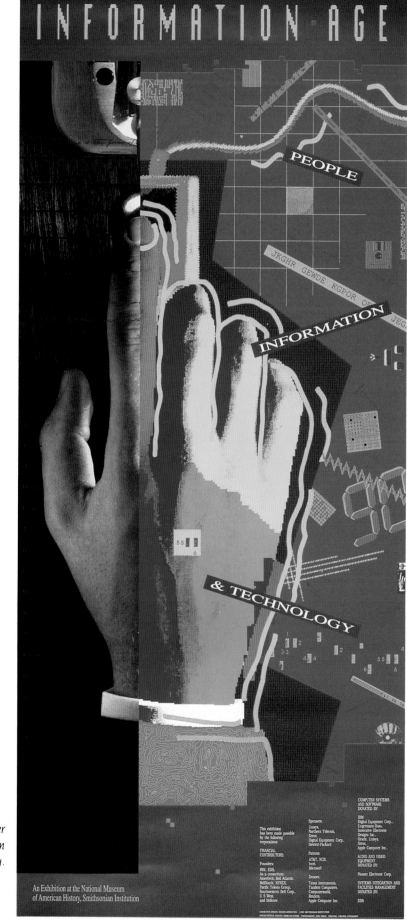

Senior citizens housing brochure for B'nai B'rith.

Then she learned the software business inside and out. The extensive local group of software development and engineering firms were impressed when they found someone who understood the term "fourth-generation language." Today, "we're a large-scale design house that's not an ad agency," Kirpich explains. "Many of our customers won't choose a two or three-person shop because they aren't sure if they'll get the service they want. Our clients want to be involved in the process."

"I believe the essential ingredient to being a good designer and manager is a broad education and the need to be out there in the world. You need experiences to bring to the board. I advocate that my staff develop strong extracurricular interests. For example, one of my employees also sings on Broadway. I feel you should read the history of the world as well as the history of design."

Annual report for Systems Center, Inc.

JUDY KIRPICH

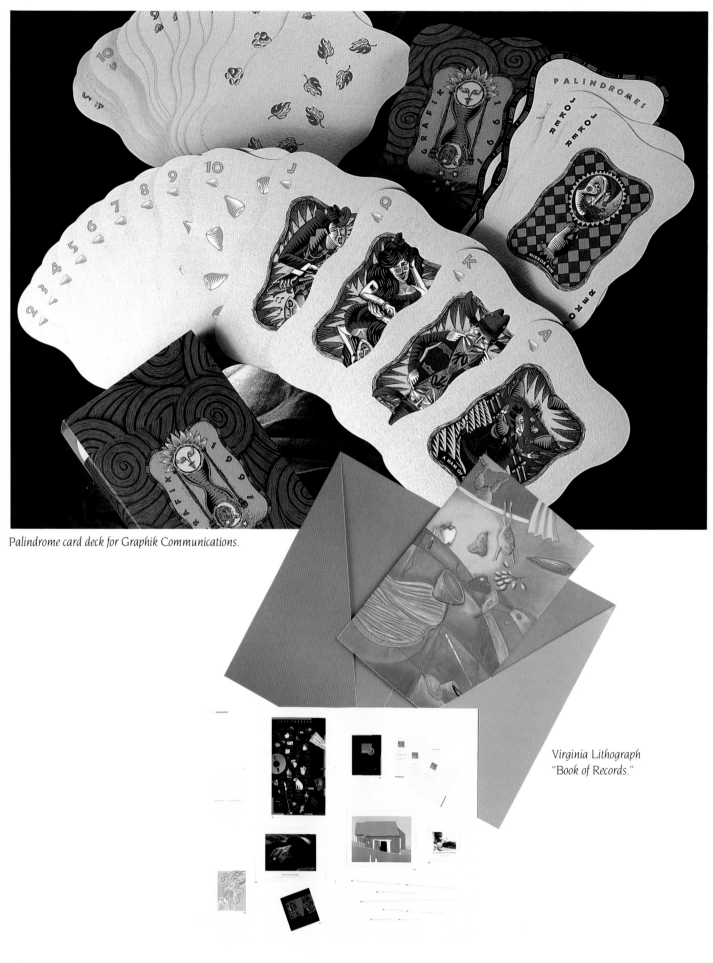

Palindrome card deck for Graphik Communications.

Virginia Lithograph
"Book of Records."

Poster for exhibit of Hollywood memorabilia.

She considers the personality and egos of potential staff members when she interviews. "At Grafik, the junior members' opinions count as much as the seniors'. I wanted this to be a place where I would want to come to during the day." It worked — Kirpich's studio enjoys consistently low turnover, where an average employee stays eight to 10 years. "I also wanted a place where women could work and be mothers, so I built flexibility into the daily routine. Working moms have a lot to figure out in this society. We need to develop systems where women can be great designers, but don't have to lose themselves either in motherhood or design." Maternity leave is generous: six months.

But, with a 20-person staff, it hasn't always been easy. "It's hard to maintain openness, especially when the country is in a recession. This is not an inexpensive way to work. I haven't always been able to keep the philosophy of the studio alive, but I'm always trying."

SONSOLES LLORENS

Sonsoles Llorens Design
Barcelona, Spain

Barcelona has a colorful history in the art industry. Picasso, Dali and Gaudí called it home. The 1992 Olympics focused the attention of the modern world directly on this graceful city and its fresh style of graphic arts. These days, the population is heavily composed of designers and artists, and children are raised with a creative sensibility. Some say that Barcelona represents the future of design in Europe.

1991 *Self-promotional New Year's cards.*

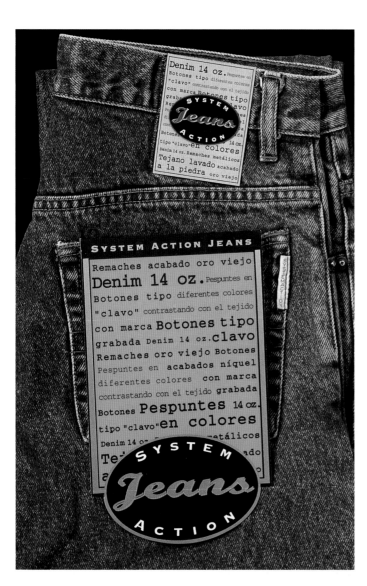

In-store tags for System Action clothing.

Spring catalog for System Action clothing.

It was in this handsome, forward-looking city that Sonsoles Llorens was born in 1961. She studied philosophy at the University of Barcelona — mostly western literature, the Greeks, classical theory. She founded her own studio in 1988. She collaborated on a variety of projects with such industry leaders as Mariscal and Núñez. She is thoroughly content with her choice of career and doesn't talk much about the future; she is much too happy with the way things are going today.

SONSOLES LLORENS

"I have tried to make my work a marriage of philosophy and design. I want to say something people understand, and I use type and color, and play with them. What makes my design unique is that I am unique. Every person is different."

Llorens' own philosophy is simple and direct. "I think you should give a good deal of thought to what you want to do and then do it," she asserts. "If what you want to do is graphic design, then do not hold yourself back. Before entering the design world, I studied philosophy for three years because I was interested in concepts, their rationalization process and speech. Now I also deal with form and color — and it's much more fun!"

Logo, letterhead, and shopping bag for Arropa, a casual clothing store.

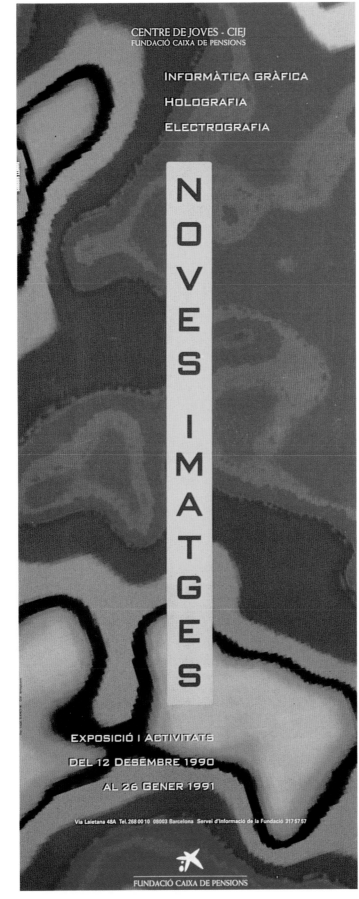

CENTRE DE JOVES - CIEJ
FUNDACIÓ CAIXA DE PENSIONS

INFORMÀTICA GRÀFICA

HOLOGRAFIA

ELECTROGRAFIA

NOVES IMATGES

EXPOSICIÓ I ACTIVITATS

DEL 12 DESÉMBRE 1990

AL 26 GENER 1991

Via Laietana 48A Tel. 268 00 10 08003 Barcelona Servei d'Informació de la Fundació 317 57 57

FUNDACIÓ CAIXA DE PENSIONS

Poster for "Exposició i Activitats
Noves Imatges," an exhibit of graphic,
holographic, and computer art.

"Success is defined as doing what you want to do, and doing it well. I like doing what I do. I want to keep improving every day, by learning new things from all people, the clients, the printers, everyone that makes up the project. I enjoy making a living with these skills." Llorens works with only one assistant in her studio, and doesn't want her business to grow much larger than that. "I want to follow the work from the beginning to the end."

"I believe color treatment is one of my strengths," Llorens says, ranking it as the fourth step in a design process that starts with listening to the client until she completely understands his or her needs and can define the project's concept to her satisfaction. "I believe form and color have a logical reading, like words. My profession is similar to talking. For example, when you speak to a child, you use certain words. But when you speak to a doctor, you use another set of words. You may say things differently, but you use the same materials."

SONSOLES LLORENS

VILLE DE MARSEILLE
SERVICES DES AFFAIRES CULTURELLES
14 RUE BEAUVAU 13001 MARSEILLE
TEL: 91 541000 FAX: 91 552484

BIENNALE DES JEUNES
CRÉATEURS D'EUROPE
DE LA MÉDITERRANÉE

MARSEILLE 1990

MARSEILLE 1990

BIENNALE DES JEUNES CRÉATEURS
D'EUROPE DE LA MÉDITERRANÉE

BIENNALE DES JEUNES
CRÉATEURS D'EUROPE
DE LA MÉDITERRANÉE

MARSEILLE 1990

VILLE DE MARSEILLE
SERVICES DES AFFAIRES CULTURELLES
14 RUE BEAUVAU 13001 MARSEIL E
TEL: 91 541000 FAX: 91 552484

Llorens lived in London for a year, and found the experience uplifting. "I have been fortunate to have traveled a little, and worked with people I admired. I love Barcelona and I want to stay here and work in my business. The environment here is good for graphic designers. It is a popular profession and a lot of young people are now interested in it."

"I get my ideas from logical thinking," she says. "I think education, experience and culture are needed for designers to be successful, both personally and professionally speaking. I don't think education is always found in schooling — you can learn from books as well, although it is slower. The important thing is to become involved in culture."

Stationery and signage for Biennale des Jeunes Créateurs d'Europe de la Méditerranée.

SONSOLES LLORENS

Letterhead and brochure for Tenispaña, the commercial division of the Royal Spanish Tennis Federation.

It's difficult to get Llorens to admit to a preference in her work. "I am lucky because I am interested in anything that has to do with design. My favorite type of work is posters and logos." She may eventually go back to school, and is not afraid to experiment with computers and software. "I'm ready to buy any technical

device which will help me improve my design process." And she believes there is strength in numbers. "I have good friends in the design world. I believe unity gives strength, so I therefore believe in industry associations. Awards, too, are important. They help us to know what others are doing."

Poster and T-shirt promoting the Spain vs. Israel Davis Cup elimination round.

NORA OLGYAY

Foci Studio
Washington, D.C., USA

Nora Olgyay says things like, "Designers have a lot to contribute to the world," and means them. "The design process is unique and valuable because it doesn't assume what the end result will be," she explains. "I think such a way of thinking would be helpful in other intellectual endeavors, such as medical research."

Promotional brochure for ANA's (All Nippon Airways) Pacific Bonus Program.

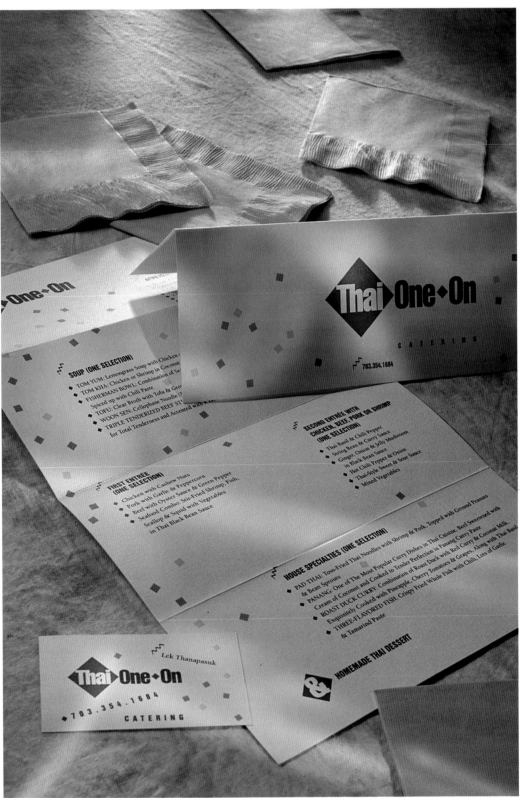

Identity, stationery, and collateral pieces for Thai-One-On, a Thai food caterer.

Olgyay, principal of Foci Studio, has a warm place in her heart for the medical field. "The other career I considered was medicine," a choice she sometimes recalls wistfully because of what she calls "the credibility gap." "I have strong beliefs and visions for the world. Designers are usually not perceived as legitimate contributors to society, the way doctors are, for example. In the eyes of the public, sometimes being a doctor automatically makes you an expert on everything else as well!"

NORA OLGYAY

Stationery, announcement, and marketing materials for LeMay Associates, an architectural firm.

Olgyay is primarily an environmental graphic designer, a field devoted to the planning, design and execution of graphic elements in the built and natural environment. It's a field she stumbled upon while doing civil rights work, which fit perfectly with her desire to explore ways to make the world more responsive to human needs. Her extensive experience qualifies her as an expert in environmental design, and she had been quoted in publications from *The Wall Street Journal* to *Identity Magazine*. She speaks about her work with pure happiness and energy, enthusiastic about the effort to support the disabled, senior citizens and the general public.

"Our design solutions involve making spaces and information accessible through effective integration of landscaping, architecture, lighting and environmental graphic design." A Princeton graduate, she is the recipient of a National Endowment for the Arts grant to develop and test a set of national standard hazard warning symbols. She is also very goal-oriented.

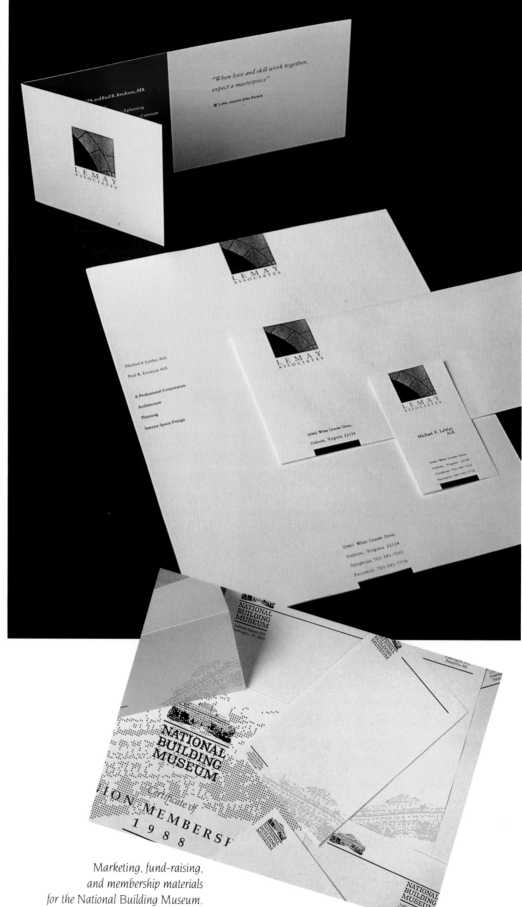

Marketing, fund-raising, and membership materials for the National Building Museum.

"Creating the Southeast Federal Center," a condensation of a formal, five-volume government development proposal.

Design and implementation of the environmental graphics of London's Canary Wharf development.

"The primary focus of my work is to foster accessibility — both physical and cognitive — to the environment," states this American University adjunct professor, who lists her interests as community activism and civil rights. The easiest thing about that mission is understanding the challenge. "The most difficult is meeting that challenge."

NORA OLGYAY

Signage standards program for one of BDM Corporation's regional headquarters.

But which is the most enjoyable? "Problem-solving," she laughs, "so I guess I enjoy the hardest part of my work the best."

But that goes with her nature. "If I knew exactly what to expect every day from nine to five, I wouldn't want to be doing it. Graphic art offers risks. If you enjoy the unknown, you may do well in this field. If you want emotional and financial certainty in your life, don't become a designer."

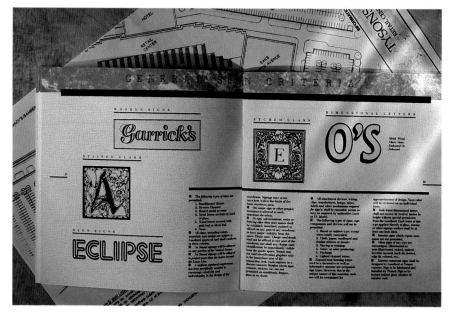

Architectural design criteria manual for retail tenants of The Tysons II Galleria.

Identity and architectural graphics for Washington, D.C.'s Van Ness Station.

"Collaboration — with experts in various other fields as well as with other designers — is an integral part of my work. Memberships and conferences are an important part of that."

She still sees challenges in her field. "I don't completely agree with the criteria for design awards. I think they should expand the criteria to include effective information and services to the public. A lawyer knows when he or she has achieved success because the case is either won or lost. Markers aren't as clear for designers. A design could work well for a client but never win an award because it doesn't measure up in the current categories."

Interior signage for a regional headquarters of McGraw-Hill, Inc.

Fund-raising poster and tabletop display for a soup kitchen.

NORA OLGYAY

Draft spread and sketches from the book Safety Symbols: A National System.

The visible text within the draft spread reads:

...fied system of comprehensible, tested and ...udience exposure, improve comprehension ...reby enhance worker and public safety, ...for applications to safety signs, labels, tags ...4 permitted without written permission of ...ats which present comprehensive ...e of flux of standards for safety ...lication of the symbols. Safety ...abrication materials, text, color ...national, national and international ...SI Z535 standard itself has three separate ...ls or tags. The reader is advised to refer to ...the 40 different safety messages identified ...r to present the most effective set of safety ...mon borders and standardized elements.

the worker is gaining the experience and knowledge to navigate the particular environment, and that the incidence of injury and illness decreases with length of service. Familiarity with the workplace is an

essential safety component. Yet the workforce is increasingly transient and the technology ever-changing. As a consequence, safety and hazard warning messages may be

¶ The symbol system includes fifteen symbols for "hazard warning": Biohazard, Corrosion, Cut/Sever, Electrical, Electrical/Hand, Entanglement, Explosion, Fall, Flammable, Hot Surface, Laser, Pinch, Poison, Radiation, Radio Frequency, Safety Alert, Slip and Trip. The eight "mandatory actions" include: Ear Protection, Eye Protection, Foot Protection, Hand Protection, Head Protection, Respiratory Protection/Air Line, Respiratory Protection/Mask and Respiratory Protection/Respirator. The seven symbols for "prohibited actions" are Do Not Touch, No Entrance/People, No Entrance/Vehicles, No Exit, No Open Flame/Match, No Open Flame/Flame and No Smoking. The seven "general safety messages" include Direction, Eye Wash, Exit, Extinguisher, Fire Hose & Reel, First Aid and Safety Shower. Art for more than one version of a symbol is included if there are varying application requirements. ¶ All symbols are presented with a surround shape as an integral part of the symbol. Although a few standards do allow the use of safety symbols without a surround shape, it is generally discouraged. Surround shapes are recognized by both ISO and ANSI as offering valuable visual cues which provide supportive information about the nature of the safety message. The surround shapes presented with the SEGD symbols match the ANSI Z535 requirements and those of ISO, except that ISO does not recognize the use of a diamond as a surround shape for safety signs. The diamond surround shape is presented here and in Z535 as an option to the use of a triangle for hazard alert symbols. Testing by the US Bureau of Standards has proven that the diamond shape is equally recognized in the US as a hazard warning and that *the diamond shape increases legibility because it allows the symbol located inside it to be larger than in the same size triangle.* Consequently art for all SEGD

"In fact, I hope society will eventually broaden its entire definition of success. Instead of desensitizing both women and men to thinking success must always include wealth or prestige or leisure, the formula should respond to individual needs. The classic formula for success often cuts women out."

Olgyay's current project is an ongoing effort to achieve balance in her life. "One of the drawbacks to loving your work as much as I do is that it leaves too little time for your personal life. I'm working on remedying that."

Proposed information pylons for Philadephia's 30th Street Train Station.

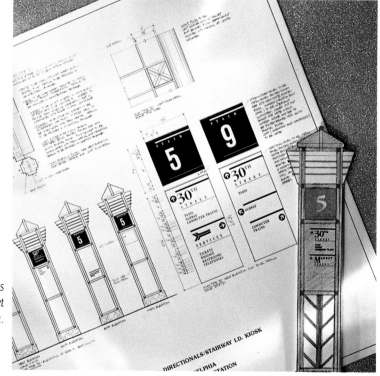

Standardized icons from the book Safety Symbols: A National System.

PAULA SCHER

Pentagram
New York, New York, USA

When we first spoke with Paula Scher, we asked her what she did best. "I make very good, continual, dumb, irrelevant jokes," she said.

As a literary designer (i.e., "I write and read and make analogies"), she has been called a vanishing breed. "The analogy is the important part — connecting words and images that have another meaning." She's written two books (*The Honeymoon Book* and *The Brownstone*), writes her own copy and has had articles published in magazines from *Adweek* to *Print*. Scher admits to a deep respect for early

Packaging for nuts and popcorn for Oola candy stores.

öola

20th-century design. But "the problem with my work is that it needs captions," she maintains, although few of her peers would see that as a problem. "You have to read the lines to know what it's about. If you simply look at the work, you may not have any idea of why I did it that way. A great deal of my work is specifically related to the copy."

Store front of Oola candy store.

*Shopping bags for
Oola candy stores.*

PAULA SCHER

Scher has been designing for 20 years now. "Your age affects the way you approach a project. You make mistakes when you're young, but you also make incredible discoveries that become part of your vocabulary and a piece of your knowledge. The older you get, the more you know, but that knowledge prevents that 'accident' from occurring. You lose that innocence. Knowledge makes you more facile at solving problems, but you won't make that great mistake." We asked Scher what design piece has given her the greatest satisfaction. "The one I haven't done yet," she answered.

Born in Washington, D.C., Scher received a BFA from the Tyler School of Art. Her grandfather was a photographer and her father worked with the U.S. Geological Survey. "There were always great maps around the house." She started out as an illustrator, but soon excelled at designing book and record covers, magazines and packaging. Scher spent many years as an art director for CBS Records, where her work won accolades and four Grammy nominations. She got out of the music business in 1982, and she and Terry Koppel founded Koppel & Scher in 1984. She later became a consultant, and then in 1991, accepted a partnership in Pentagram.

Poster for inaugural party of Bard College's Center for Curatorial Studies.

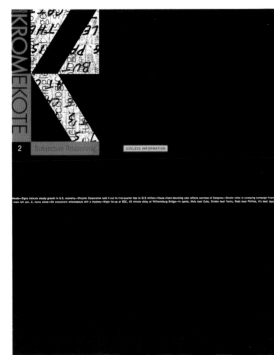

Cover and spreads from "Useless Information,"
part of a promotional series for
Champion International Corporation's
Kromekote paper.

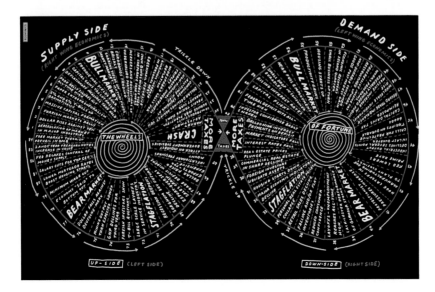

PAULA SCHER

"My professional priorities are tied to my personal priorities. The relationship with the client is important — assessing and filling a need, translating the information. It's a clear relationship, but I'm always personally trying to grow within it, trying to do it in a new way. The notion of change is important, as in changing a form."

"Most of the people whose design I admire are those whose work only they can do," Scher notes. "At one time, I thought I should make an alphabetized thank-you list to all the people who I admire, personally and professionally. People like Woody Allen, Humphrey Bogart, George Carlin — there are many inspirations, and when I love them, I really love them. I love 1930s movies from Warner Brothers Pictures. And I'm a great fan of my husband. He's a terrific designer and illustrator."

In-store display for UVU, a television set by RCA (Thompson Consumer Electronics).

Boxes as point-of-purchase display for UVU.

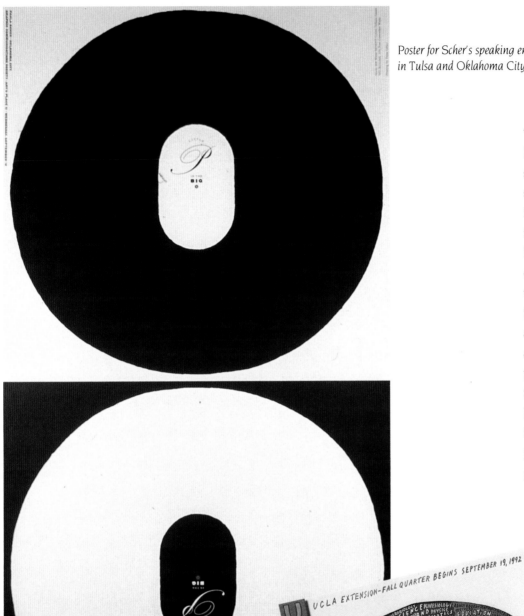

Poster for Scher's speaking engagements in Tulsa and Oklahoma City, Oklahoma.

"Being a woman in business is like being in a very low-security prison." Scher is serious, but there is empathy in her tone. "You think you're free, but you run into a blockade you didn't see or expect, and you must find a way around it. And it goes on forever. It's important to acknowledge the barriers exist, and to accept that. And then you must find away around it." She is not discouraged by the hurdles, and refuses to point fingers. "Barriers are not built just by men; women still participate, too."

Cover for the 1992 Extension Catalog of the University of California at Los Angeles.

PAULA SCHER

Long box, CD, and booklet
for Bob James and Earl Klugh,
Warner Bros. Records.

She has taught a Senior
Portfolio course at the School
of Visual Arts in New York.
"When you have the energy to
teach — and it takes a lot of
energy — you can get back so
much more than you give."
Scher got a lot back by
watching her students
improve. "I had them look at
each individual piece and
figure out why it didn't work.
Then they determined how to
make it better. The evolution
of each piece was magical.
Teaching exercises my design
ability — we deal with scale,
proportion and all the rest,
and to be able to see those
components work is exciting."
She also holds small design
classes in her studio.

1 Movin' On
2 As It Happens
3 So Much In
  Common
4 Fugitive Life
5 The Night That
  Love Came Back
6 Secret Wishes
7 New York Samba
8 Handara
9 The Sponge
10 Terpsichore
11 San Diego Stomp
12 Miniature

Produced by
Earl Klugh and
Bob James

DDD

COMPACT DISC
DIGITAL AUDIO

WB

0 7599-26939-2 9

SCHOOL OF VISUAL ARTS ⓢⓥⓐ A COLLEGE OF THE ARTS

GREAT IDEAS NEVER HAPPEN WITHOUT IMAGINATION

Subway and bus shelter poster for the School of Visual Arts.

What's in the future — more books? "*Honeymoon* is about the origins of honeymoons, rituals, celebrity honeymoons, all that sort of thing. I wrote it by request, and because it offered a big advance." She laughs. "Anytime I make a decision based only on money, it has failed. I am much better at writing satire." What new projects would she like to try? "Three-dimensional work. I'd like to design furniture. Right now, I love posters — the bigger, the better. My favorite work is packaging. I'm looking for larger projects. I've learned that if something looks big and ugly, it's because it's not big enough."

Cover for the 1991 Annual of the American Institute of Graphic Arts.

GRAPHIC DESIGN U.S.A. 11

ELLEN SHAPIRO

Shapiro Design Associates, Inc.
New York, New York, USA

"Too many designers don't care enough about the words, only about the visuals," notes Ellen Shapiro, who is known to spend two hours perfecting a paragraph for a clients' ad or brochure. The principal of New York's Shapiro Design Associates, Inc. founded her design and communications firm in 1978, and now touts a long list of accomplishments and blue chip client list.

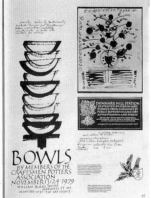

Cover and spread of Upper and Lower Case (U&lc).

Custom patient menus for
*Beth Israel Medical Center's Food
and Nutrition Service.*

*Development brochure for The Singers Forum, a vocal arts
school and performance center.*

Throughout Shapiro's career, her errors and those of her competitors were great teachers. The most common complaint she has heard from dissatisfied clients is that designers don't care about solving the client's problem — only about doing what they think will win awards. "For me," Shapiro says, "visual communication is mostly about being a producer. I try to keep it simple, elegant, fresh and memorable, all at once." She tries not to worry about important finishing touches — like color or paper stock — until the problem is solved conceptually. She maintains that a solution that doesn't work in black and white probably can't be saved by color. "And you have to know exactly what you want. That may take years of experience."

ELLEN SHAPIRO

One of a rare breed of designers who copywrites almost all her projects, Shapiro has also contributed articles to publications like The American Institute of Graphic Arts' *Journal*, *Communication Arts* and *Print*. She has taught corporate identity — with an emphasis on substance and message as well as aesthetics — at Pratt Institute and Parsons School of Design.

But it is possible to pack Shapiro's diverse personality into a word or two. Detail-oriented. Serious. Demanding. Maybe even compulsive. She says some people tell her to lighten up. But her intense attitude has earned her staying power in the Big Apple and the industry. "My clients have learned, I think, that they can trust me."

Identity program, including annual report and "Op-Ed" advertising, for United Hospital Fund.

Channeling Children's Anger

*Identity for "Channeling Children's Anger,"
a conference and public service television campaign
for the Institute for Mental Health Initiatives.*

Education has been influential. "The teacher who made the most difference in my life, John Neuhart, used to say, 'The designer has a responsibility to society to determine how things look.' My favorite classes at the University of California at Los Angeles were African history, literary criticism, theater design, Shakespeare, and philosophy. African history seemed like a good idea in 1968 because my boyfriend at the time had just left for the Peace Corps in the Ivory Coast. In my first class, I discovered a continent and people whose accomplishments had clearly, deliberately and criminally been left out of 'world history.' I studied hard and became an editorial assistant on African Arts magazine, and worked my way through college on that part-time salary."

ELLEN SHAPIRO

"Establishment Services Communication Guidelines" for American Express.

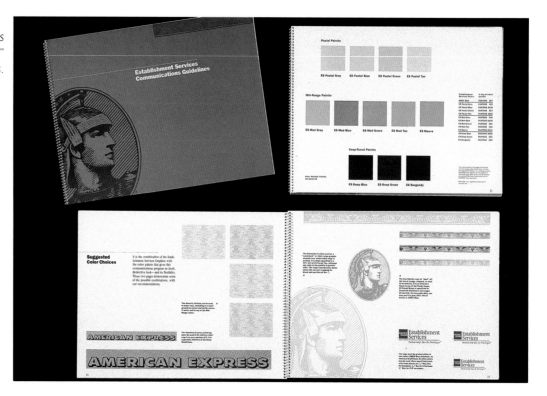

By the mid 1980s, Shapiro was managing ten employees, and thought that, in order to attract and keep leading corporate clients, it was necessary to build a large office on a prime piece of Manhattan real estate. She commissioned architects to design her new headquarters from scratch. Then came the 1987 stock market crash, which caused many of her clients to make big cutbacks in their design budgets. And almost every month, she struggled to meet overheard costs. Today, she works out of a more modest office with only one or two full-time assistants and uses freelancers. "I am happier, less anxious. Things seem in balance." "My clients are actually happier because I'm the one doing most of the work."

Directory of Manhattan restaurants welcoming the American Express® Card.

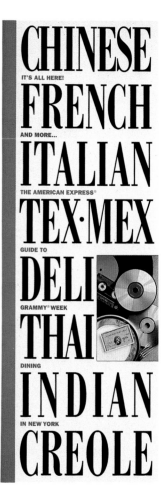

CHINESE
IT'S ALL HERE!
FRENCH
AND MORE...
ITALIAN
THE AMERICAN EXPRESS®
TEX·MEX
GUIDE TO
DELI
GRAMMY® WEEK
THAI
DINING
INDIAN
IN NEW YORK
CREOLE

Clients and Designers, *a book by Ellen Shapiro.*

Logo for "Bouncing Back," an educational
program sponsored by the Institute
for Mental Health Initiatives.

Shapiro maintains that beginning graphic artists should also pay attention to the business end of the industry. "Learn how to write proposals and use time sheets. Study type books and paper samples at home, read The Wall Street Journal — the more you know, the more you are worth."

ELLEN SHAPIRO

The Shapiro talent is not confined to design. She cooks, gardens and throws a mean party. Having successfully completed the renovation and interior design of her 1960s modernist home — down to the faucets, knobs and tiles — Shapiro wonders about getting into some residential interiors commissions. She is interested in black-and-white photography. She thinks about working on a television commercial, a film or a video.

Ad campaign for Century Time Ltd., makers of hand-faceted, sapphire watches.

Capabilities brochure for International Typeface Corporation.

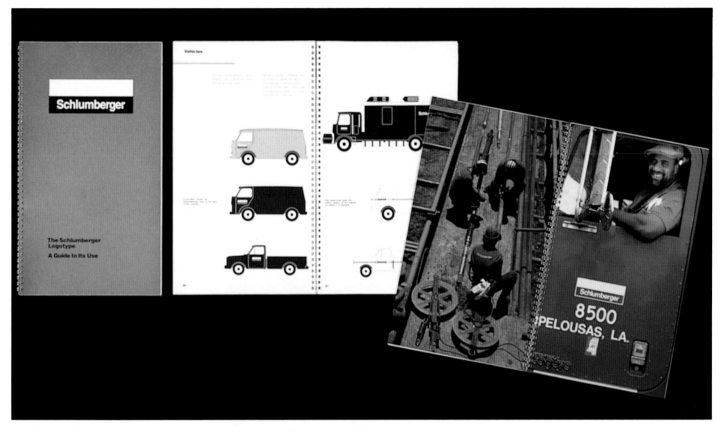

Identity guidelines for Schlumberger Ltd., multinational oil drilling and exploration corporation.

She fantasizes about starting a cooking magazine called Bold Knife and Fork: The Magazine for Adventurous Eaters. When she has a few free moments, however, chances are you'll find her writing fiction. "That's where a new creative interest lies now," she says.

Annual report for Electro-Biology, Inc., manufacturer of electronic bone-healing equipment.

LORI SIEBERT

Siebert Design
Cincinnati, Ohio, USA

"I've taken painting and drawing classes since the age of seven," says Lori Siebert in a quiet voice that combines a sense of self-confidence with respectful humility towards her success. "I guess a graphic arts career chose me."

Materials for the "Hewlett-Packard Peripherals Developers Conference '92."

Brochure for Jack Rouse Associates.

She started Siebert Design Associates in a 10' X 12' office suite three years out of college and has been busy ever since, striving to consistently create design that "communicates messages, feelings or impressions in a simple, clear, uncluttered way."

"I'm an excellent listener with a great love of design. During the first stage of my work, I try to hear what my customers tell me, both in words and through their inflection and gestures. The second stage is the thinking process, and the third is creative. I don't think you can be successful if you emphasize the creative side of graphics and ignore the analytical."

"City Shapes" edition of Printing by Design.

LORI SIEBERT

To support the thinking process, Siebert located her business within walking distance from the library. It's here that the most difficult part of the process — the birth of an idea — takes place. "I look through history books, art books, books that are not even related to the project. I start to build on ideas by writing word associations. Then I develop a picture list of images associated with the concept I'm trying to explain." For example, one of her clients, a media buyer, prided itself on its hands-on, down-to-earth approach, even to the point of locating its headquarters inside an old schoolhouse. Their style said "homespun" to Siebert. So she researched folk art and found books illustrating antique cigarette trading cards. These are the images which will find themselves part of the company's identity.

"I'm motivated by love, money and power, in that order," she says. "But love is complex — to me, it means both love of work and love of family. Both are necessary to keep my life happy and balanced. And I believe if you truly love your work, the money and power will follow."

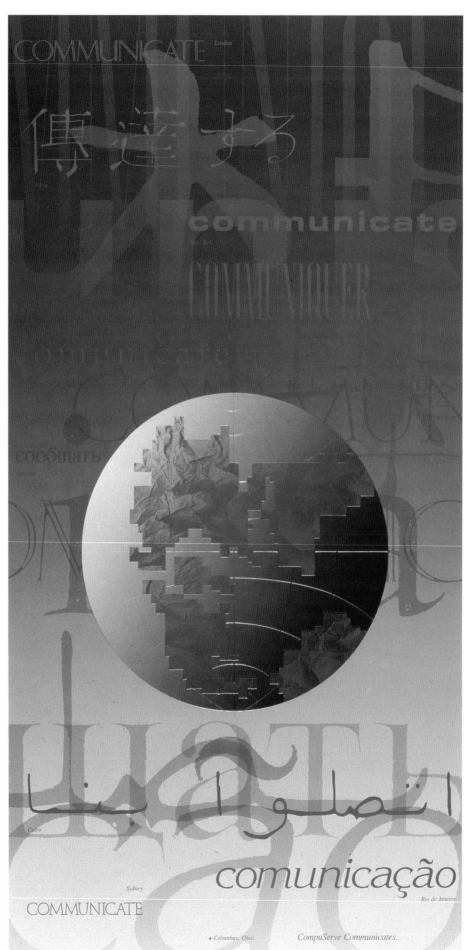

Poster on communication for CompuServe.

Poster, notecard, and stationery line entitled
"Wild about the World."

Stationery for Jean Cecil Gilliam, Inc.,
architect and interior designer.

LORI SIEBERT

"Formations" brochure for Formica Corporation.

Siebert, whose eclectic design has been featured at the Akron Art Museum, has few complaints — perhaps a little more travel, a little more leisure time with her child and her husband Steve, now a full-time employee of the firm. "He does the accounting and holds down the fort," she says, freeing her for volunteer work at the Ensemble Theater in Cincinnati, the American Institute of Graphic Artists, and the Children's Dental Care Foundation. Siebert designs print material for the Foundation, which provides free dental care for needy families.

Identity system for retailer Rags 2 Riches.

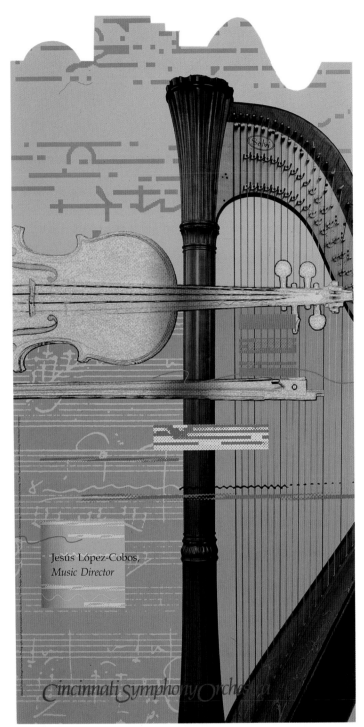

Posters for the Cincinnati Symphony and Pops Orchestras.

LORI SIEBERT

"I hope my next accomplishment will be to work with a fairly obscure, upstart company, perhaps in the fashion or furniture industry, and, with effective graphics, play a big role in its success." These days, she socializes when she can with other designers — "I learn so much from them, and they have a good sense of humor" — and is a member of the informal "Women's Club," a group of women designers who meet monthly for lunch and end up talking "about everything but design."

"Most of the designers I know who are women think of themselves as 'designers,' not 'women designers,' because design isn't gender-oriented."

She's concerned that technology is being misused. "Design has become so complex, it challenges the public to understand its meaning. This is partially due to the popularity of the computer. I'm concerned when the co-op students with whom we work skip the thinking process and head right for the computers. It shows in their work, and I often have to caution them: 'it looks beautiful, but where's the idea?'"

Series of notecards for Good Nature Designs.

Annual report for Mercy Health System.

Brochure for FINIS, a post production company for film and video.

Stationery system for FINIS.

"Anyone can design well if you are passionate about your work, ask a lot of questions, learn from everyone you can and gather information from various sources. At the end of all that, make sure you find your own way of doing things. Design is an immensely personal art."

CATHERINE LAM SIU-HUNG

Cat Lam Design
Hong Kong, Hong Kong

"**S**uccess," says Catherine Lam Siu-hung, a.k.a. Cat Lam and Cat Production, "is the transcendence of the limits of your mind, so that you achieve something beyond your imagination." Anyone who has seen Lam's 1989 "horoscope symbols" identity campaign will understand what she means by "beyond imagination." "Among my works, the 'horoscope symbols' are my favorite to date," Lam says. "This work reflects the lovely cartoon images I saw when I was still young, combined with bits and pieces of interesting things I encountered during childhood. I tried to create this series of symbols with a touch of innocence and purity."

Christmas card for Triumph International (HK) Ltd.

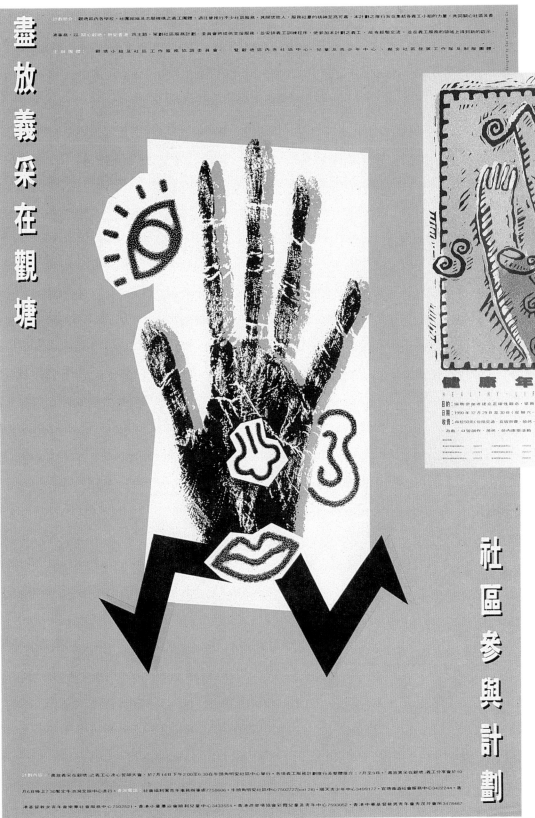

Lam has encountered many "interesting things" in her very short but remarkable career. She received her diploma in graphic design from the Sha Tin Technical Institute in 1989, and worked with some of the most famous design firms in the Far East, including Alan Chan Design, before establishing Cat Lam Design in 1990. Her artwork has been featured in a variety of books, including *International Logos and Trademarks* (U.S.A.) and *Famous Animal Symbols* (Belgium). She already has a list of design awards to her credit. And we found her to be a patient person, happy to help Americans who spoke not a word of her language.

CATHERINE LAM SIU-HUNG

Aquarius

Pisces

ARIES

Taurus

Gemini

CANCER

Leo

Virgo

Libra

SCORPIO

Sagittarius

Capricorn

Horoscope icons for Art Gallery.

Horoscope postcards
for Art Gallery.

She is methodical on the job. "When I begin a graphics project, I first study the nature of the product or service. I then try to decide which method of design will best represent the intrinsic quality of the product." This step is the one that takes some time. Lam investigates the histories of relevant products and services and their promotional strategies to determine a unique way of presenting the project. "Color is a crucial element during layout preparation," she emphasizes. "Whether color applications are sufficiently impressive or presentable depends on one's choice of color combinations."

Invitation to HOM fashion show.

CATHERINE LAM SIU-HUNG

Resourceful and organized as well as creative, Lam recalls a talent for the arts was evident even while she was growing up. She attributes her creative ability to a gift of sensitivity. "I always feel the pulse of the surroundings," she explains. "I like to put down my imaginations as pictures. Maybe that's the reason that illustration was my favorite subject when I was in school."

A conversation with the soft-spoken Lam may leave an impression of a quiet, reserved woman, but her design shows the playful energy and artistic insight that are part of Lam's personality. "My works are optimistic and positive, with a touch of humor and fun. I want my audience to feel happy. I have a belief that it's a designer's responsibility to communicate with others in a positive way. I love to immerse myself into my works spiritually."

Promotional poster for STAR TV, China.

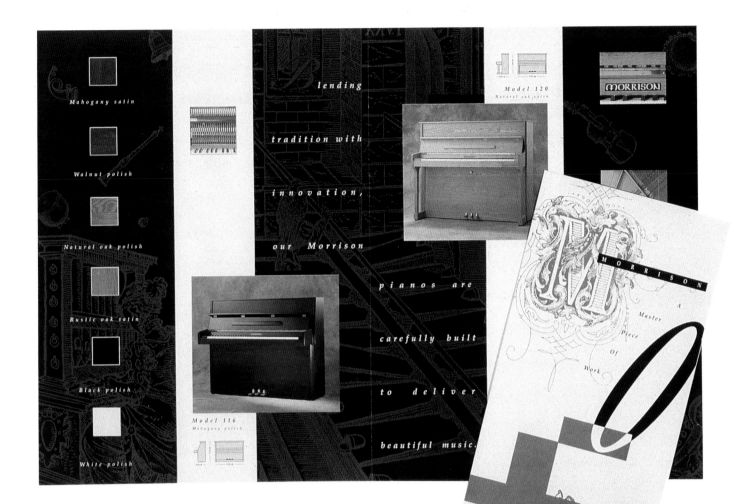

Mahogany satin

Walnut polish

Natural oak polish

Rustic oak satin

Black polish

White polish

Model 116
Mahogany polish

ᗷ lending

tradition with

innovation,

our Morrison

pianos are

carefully built

to deliver

beautiful music.

Model 120
Natural oak satin

MORRISON

MORRISON

A
Master
Piece
Of
Work

From

TSANG FOOK PIANO CO

"Morrison" brochure
for Tsang Fook
Piano Company.

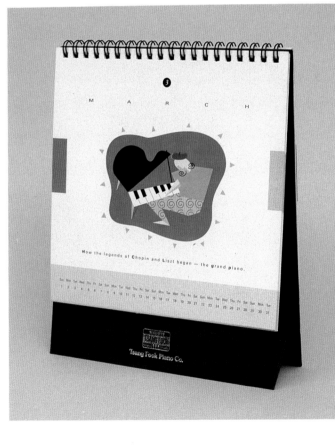

Desktop calendar for
Tsang Fook Piano Company.

CATHERINE LAM SIU-HUNG

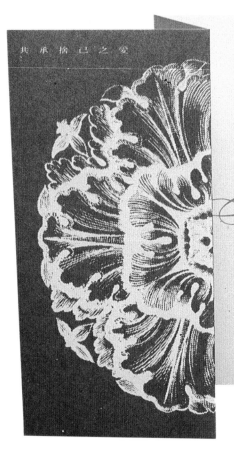

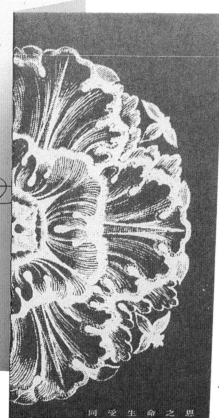

共 承 捨 己 之 愛

我倆謹訂於

主曆一九九一年七月二十日

（星期六）下午二時正假座

九龍亞皆老街206號

九龍城浸信會

舉行結婚典禮

誠意邀請 • 同頌主恩

盧智棠 • 黃穎兒

敬約

禮成敬備茶點

同 受 生 命 之 恩

Wedding card.

"Sometimes I dream that I will have my own exhibition or even a gallery," she says. "Through these facilities, I might enhance the education of arts for people of a different culture. I would like to learn from the essence of other countries, so that my own scope of vision could be stretched. Apart from visiting those countries with long cultural histories, such as Egypt or Italy, I would also like to learn from small countries, such as Mongolia." But she intends to keep her native Hong Kong her home base. "After all, I want to contribute to my own country."

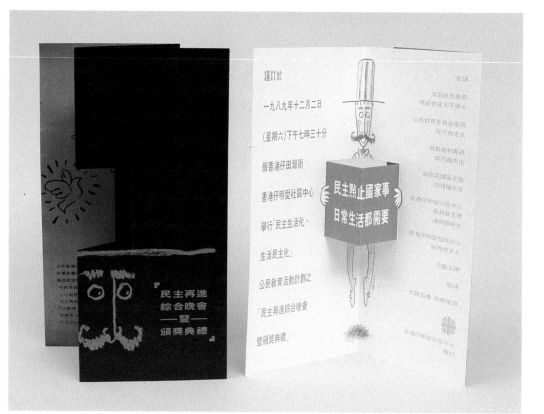

Invitation for "On Democracy," an educational campaign.

主辦機構：香港仔及海港分區委員會　　日期：一九九〇年十月二十八日（星期日）

時間：下午二時至六時　　地點：香港仔海濱公園　　節目內容：攤位遊戲．健康

展覽．幼稚園學生講故事比賽及小學生鉛筆畫比賽　　查詢電話：五五二〇九四八

香港政府印務局印

Promotional material for a children's carnival.

Lam believes she has a responsibility to children and young adults, and that motivates her work. "I will try to educate the younger generation," she says. "I wish to create something that will influence the coming generations. Certainly I'll try my best to do good for the human race. I do not want to promote bad taste or evil concepts." Lam summarizes her philosophy as "always create, never imitate." It can be a struggle. "There is nothing easy to design," she asserts. "To jump out of prevailing trends is the most difficult part."

"Design is a challenging career," maintains Lam. "But it can bring forward the creativity embedded inside my mind, release it, make things happen. Each time I develop a new design, I hope to have some sort of breakthrough. I am pleased when my works are recognized and understood by others. Fortune and glory may someday be healthy byproducts of my career."

LESLIE SMOLAN

Carbone Smolan Associates
New York, New York, USA

If you ask her, she can recite a long list of clients, and they include some heavy-hitters: The Louvre in Paris, New York's Museum of Modern Art, the American Stock Exchange, Merrill Lynch, Citicorp. Spend half an hour talking with Leslie Smolan, however, and what may impress you more is that, despite accomplishments that are the envy of many of her peers, her modesty is genuine, and refreshing. "Design is a very collaborative process," she says. "Great clients make great design. People in our office make huge contributions to our work — so much so that the problem becomes trying to acknowledge everyone enough."

The Hat Book, *a self-promotion by Carbone Smolan Associates.*

*Identity and guest amenities for
Rafael Group/Rafael Hotel.*

This New York-born principle
of Carbone Smolan Associates
feels her career combines her
intellectualism with her
artistic expression. "Design is
a commercial activity, with
marketing goals," she says. "It
involves understanding the
business aspects, and
applying intellectual activity to
that. I look for a human
common denominator in
business. It's a constant
learning experience."

LESLIE SMOLAN

"The design process hinges on reducing the message to a single idea that drives the whole project. Then you build it back up visually. You have to have something to hook onto. Looking beautiful is not enough — it's like making a suit and not fitting it to someone's body." Smolan cites the example of a company that wanted to promote its 65 different mutual funds. Carbone Smolan distilled the funds down to four investment strategies that successfully drove all the sales and product literature. And there's one more factor: "There should always be a surprise — something done a little out of the norm that makes it memorable. I want it to be something I'll still like in 10 years."

Product design and brand identity for Primis, McGraw-Hill's customized textbook series.

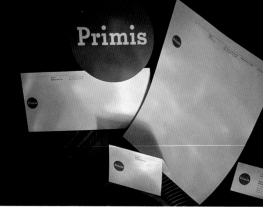

Product styling for Dansk dinnerware.

Smolan has been described as thoughtful, tough and supportive. She is an outstanding facilitator and undoubtedly a perfectionist. "I usually know when to accommodate another's viewpoint and when to stand my ground," she maintains. "When you have a large project with many personalities, you're constantly reaching a crisis point. But I know how to keep everyone moving forward as a group. I have learned how to choose the important battles."

As a young adult, Smolan wasn't isolated in an artists' community, but had broad exposure to different disciplines. "Formal education is crucial," she asserts. "The different waves of students that come into our studio show the successes and failures in the educational process. We've lately been seeing too much focus on computers, when students do not yet know how to think. One needs to conceptualize first, then use the computers as tools. Often, the schools simply need more time with the students."

LESLIE SMOLAN

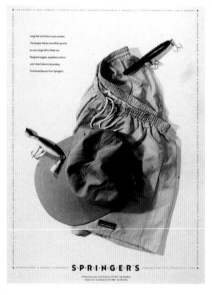

Packaging, identity, and ads for Springer's, a clothing retailer.

"Over the years, I have found that designer skills need to be as well-rounded in communications as possible. One needs to develop both strong writing and speaking skills. You need to speak well to express your presentations. I love the creative aspect of promotional writing. It shows how you think. And good drawing is essential. You must be able to draw faster than the computer."

GRAND LOUVRE

Carbone Smolan Associates
Signalétique du Grand Louvre
Programme Design

Visitor information system and signage for The Grand Louvre.

Although her family shared a passion for reading, a graphics life was hers alone. Her mother was a children's librarian and her father worked in marketing for a pharmaceutical company. But both brothers share her artistic bent: "One is a photographer, the other a filmmaker."

Smolan has strong opinions about the field of graphic art. "I wish that, as an industry, we wouldn't talk about ourselves so much. It would be nice if this wasn't so much of a beauty contest." She thinks being a woman in the business can sometimes work as an advantage. "There are so many men in graphics, I can be memorable." She supports involvement in design groups. "Memberships in organizations are important at different points in a designer's career. Shared experiences are always helpful." But she cautions that technology should be kept somewhat at bay. "The computer pushes too fast," she says, "and that inhibits creativity. It reduces cost, but pushes the quality down at the same time. Some designers think buyers won't know the difference."

LESLIE SMOLAN

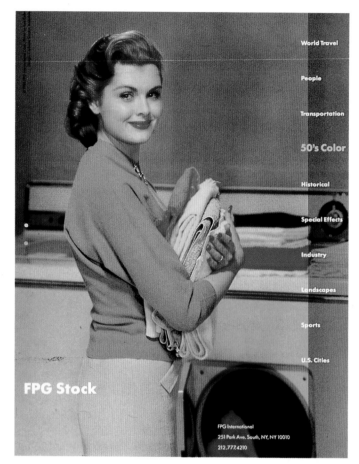

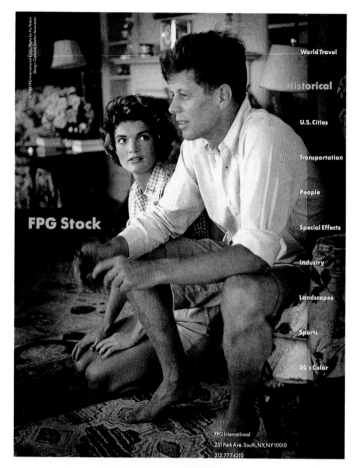

Advertising campaign for FPG Stock Photo.

"The Challenge of a New Environment"
cover for Merrill Lynch.

Catalog cover for STA 100 Show (now American Center for Design).

Her design philosophy: "Trying to make something simple is the hardest thing to do well. Society is becoming much more visual and sophisticated, making it even harder to be different. To actually make something purely distinctive is so difficult, and it never gets easier." But she hasn't yet tired of it, and calls herself "wildly optimistic" about her projects. "I'm very enthusiastic about our clients." Can she summarize the key to her success? "I think it's my partner, Ken Carbone," Smolan says, and smiles. "We've been together a long time."

Elementary textbook and marketing materials for Houghton-Mifflin's The Literature Experience.

DEBORAH SUSSMAN

Sussman / Prejza & Company, Inc.
Culver City, California, USA

Having a conversation with New York-born Deborah Sussman requires physical exertion. She talks fast, uses words that are hard to spell, and most of what she says is at the fringe of understanding. This is not because she is an intellectual elitist (on the contrary, she's quite gracious); it's because she doesn't discuss what you expect — she's already exploring a design concept unknown to most of her peers. She credits her clients and her collaborators. "They're stretching me to the next level," she says. "If you're satisfied with your work, you

Three-dimensional model of a pedestrian entry portal at Sherman Oaks Galleria, a mixed-use development.

Serpentine fence commemorating past Olympic Games.

Public food facility, one of many venues created for the 1984 Olympic Games in Los Angeles.

don't stretch anymore. I'm never satisfied. I'm always on a quest. I don't necessarily repeat the same colors again. Sometimes I'll use colors I don't even like in order to stretch."

Detail of mural in the Athletic Village at the University of California at Los Angeles.

DEBORAH SUSSMAN

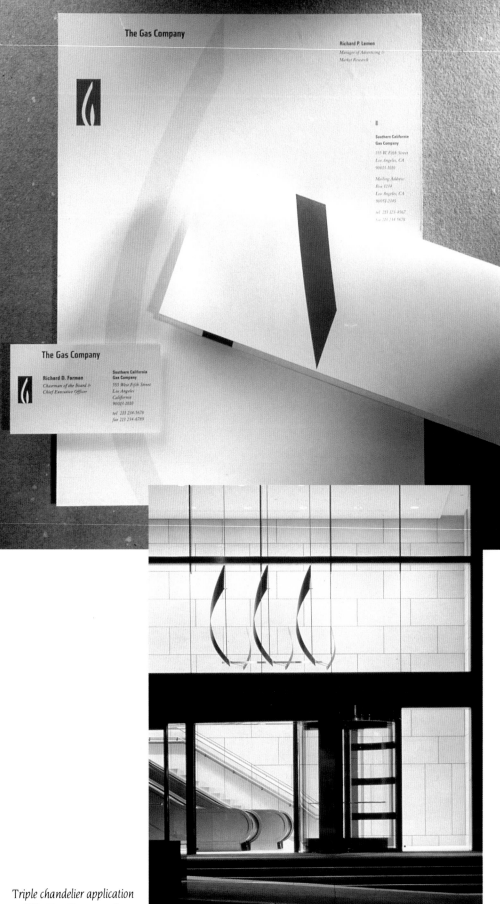

*Stationery for
The Gas Company.*

Much has been written about this half of Sussman/Prejza & Company, Inc. Sussman was schooled at Bard College, the Art Students League of New York, North Carolina's Black Mountain College and Institute of Design in Chicago. She joined the office of Charles and Ray Eames as art director, working on photography and graphic design in the early 1950s, then studied as a Fulbright Scholar in Europe. She worked as a graphic designer in Milan and Paris before she opened her own office in 1968 in Los Angeles. Then in 1980, she founded Sussman/Prejza with husband Paul and dedicated it "to the marriage of graphics and the built environment." Since then, they have developed environmental graphics for the 1984 Summer Olympics in Los Angeles, and for companies such as Hasbro, Inc., Apple Computer, Walt Disney World, EuroDisney, as well as an identity program for the Southern California Gas Company. Recently, she was honored by the Society for Environmental Graphic Design as its first woman Fellow and is an Honorary member of the American Institute of Architects.

*Triple chandelier application
of The Gas Company logo.*

Main entrance showing logo, signage, and exterior color of New Orlean's Aquarium of the Americas.

Interior of the corporate headquarters and showroom of Hasbro, Inc., a toy manufacturer.

Sussman/Prejza helped define a new discipline called "urban enhancement" — a collaboration of clients, architects and designers that enhance both the urban center and the entire streetscape. "My work attempts to integrate visual imagery with the built environment," Sussman explains. "It explores typography in time and space, in 'objects' that we work in and use in society, like buildings, and the spaces between those buildings. The spaces are the streetscape, the transportation systems — all the different ways that people interact with each other."

DEBORAH SUSSMAN

Detail of "Headdress" sculpture in the interior of Chicago Place.

We talked with Sussman during her third year of teaching at an experimental school in Santa Monica, California. "Projects evolve from my own experiences and the students' collective interests — whether that be in graphics, furniture, or painting. The separation is blurred between what is art and what is not. We're now doing site-specific pieces which each student is devising for Union Station in downtown Los Angeles, ranging from sound to sculpture to sign. I want them to think broadly. Students aren't used to thinking collaboratively."

Interior of Chicago Place, a retail center.

Exterior colors at The Citadel, a mixed-use development of a historical tire factory.

One project in collaborative thinking involved creating an alternative performance of "Peter and the Wolf." "They recomposed the music and designed the space and the performance announcement to the public."

"Currently, the office is designing a graphic / wayfinding program for Apple Computer's Research & Development Campus. We are taking Apple icons out of the computer and building them in space. It's a graphic assignment going beyond graphics, parallel to what I've given my students."

Architectural design with color, graphics, and signage at East Arcade, retail center of The Citadel.

Plaza, retail center of The Citadel.

DEBORAH SUSSMAN

EuroDisney bus.

"The most important point to me in this work is to be an artist first. That, and satisfying my clients — and their clients, the end users." Her favorite part of the design process is conceptualizing. "I'm intuitive; spontaneous, not linear. I don't like proposals and don't do them. I thrive on collaboration and teamwork. But there's still a wrestling that goes on in projects between disciplines and personalities that I find very interesting."

"Art and theater was my childhood dream," says Sussman. "I'd never retire from this career. But I hope someday to get involved with the camera again." It's not always easy. "To do what I'm doing, you should be made of cast iron. The kind of pain and abuse you have to endure as a designer — and as a female, who is not trained for battle the way men are. I've been lucky because I haven't been disadvantaged. Because my profession is important to me, I usually get respect."

Freeway sign, part of a signage program for Walt Disney World.

Directional sign for Walt Disney World.

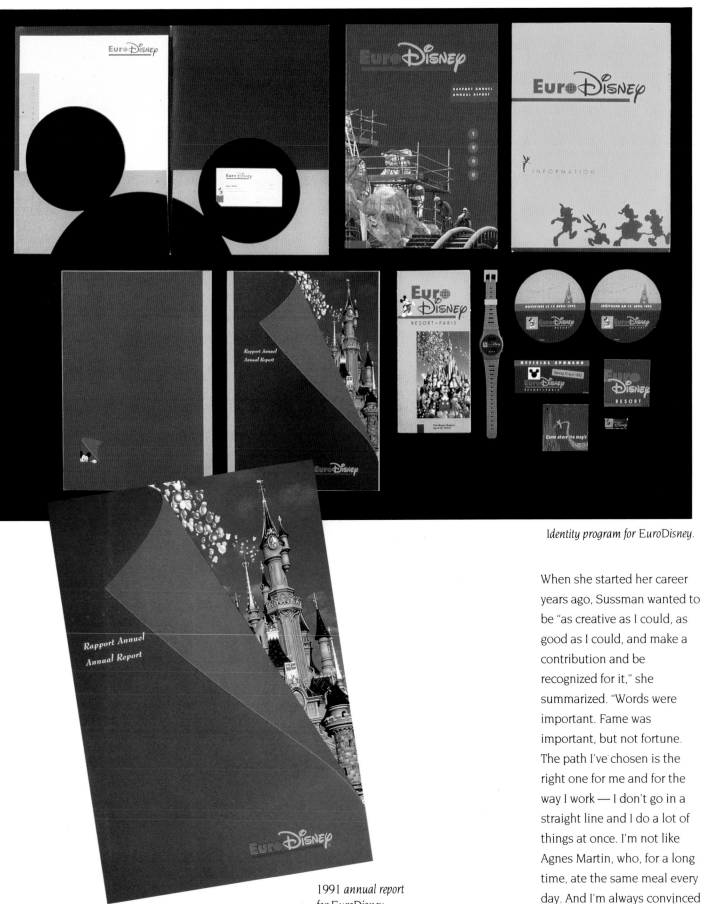

Identity program for EuroDisney.

1991 annual report for EuroDisney.

When she started her career years ago, Sussman wanted to be "as creative as I could, as good as I could, and make a contribution and be recognized for it," she summarized. "Words were important. Fame was important, but not fortune. The path I've chosen is the right one for me and for the way I work — I don't go in a straight line and I do a lot of things at once. I'm not like Agnes Martin, who, for a long time, ate the same meal every day. And I'm always convinced my next work will be better."

ROSMARIE TISSI

Odermatt & Tissi
Zurich, Switzerland

Every year, Rosmarie Tissi takes a month or two off to travel. "I unconsciously get ideas for my work by exploring new places," she says, "but I also travel for the sake of travel. That is freedom for me." She prefers the warm destinations — Asia, South America, the South Pacific. She has so far visited 65 countries. "The two most important goals for me are to enjoy life and have good work. I'd like to have money, but that is about third on my list of priorities. It is the quality of life that means most to me. As long as I can walk to the lake from my studio at lunchtime, lay in the sun or swim for an hour, I don't care about money."

Ads for a Belgian advertising magazine called Tips.

Poster for Merce Cunningham Dance Company.

She's a Swiss designer who likes to do things a little differently. "I use few elements. I remain faithful to my own philosophy but constantly renew the visual vocabulary. I strive to convey a clear statement and say a lot with a minimum of components. The traditional Swiss style is not mine, as I feel it is too heavy. My style takes some of the best attributes from the Italian style — fresh and expressive."

Tissi has 35 years of experience in the graphics industry. Her reputation is solid and, to some, enviable. In international competitions, Tissi has won first place twice, second place once, and gold and silver medals. Her work has been featured in over 30 trade magazines and books, and exhibited at the Reinhold Brown Gallery in New York, The National Museum of Modern Art in Tokyo and other esteemed locations. She has been a member of the Alliance Graphique Internationale since 1974. Tissi has lectured and juried design competitions from Germany and the United States to Japan.

ROSMARIE TISSI

Gestaltung: O&T Rosmarie Tissi

OFFSET
*Seit 1948 wandelte sich unser Betrieb
von der Buchdruckerei zu einer leistungsfähigen Offsetdruckerei. Mit einer
Vierfarbendruckmaschine, drei Zweifarbendruckmaschinen sowie drei Einfarbendruckmaschinen drucken wir bis zum
maximalen Bogenformat von 72 × 102 cm.*

*Anton Schöb
Buchdruck – Offsetdruck
Foliendruck
Birchstrasse 102
8050 Zürich
Telefon 01-311 22 60*

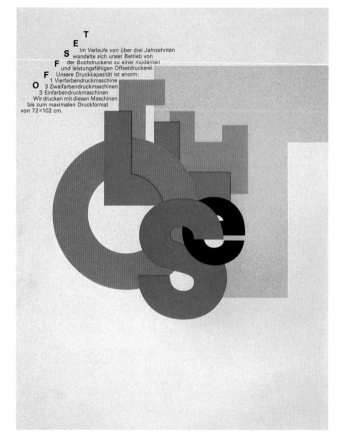

OFFSET
*Im Verlaufe von über drei Jahrzehnten
wandelte sich unser Betrieb von
der Buchdruckerei zu einer modernen
und leistungsfähigen Offsetdruckerei.
Unsere Druckkapazität ist enorm:
1 Vierfarbendruckmaschine
3 Zweifarbendruckmaschinen
3 Einfarbendruckmaschinen
Wir drucken mit diesen Maschinen
bis zum maximalen Druckformat
von 72×102 cm.*

Portfolio of posters for Offset, a printer.

She is independently spirited,
and thinks it may come from
her heritage. She comes from
a family of artists, including
architects and filmmakers. Her
uncle is a painter and her
father was a sculptor and
painter in his free time.

*Logo for Kupferschmid,
a paper dealer.*

"I advise younger people to be true to themselves in whatever career they choose. A woman working in graphic design needs to have a great deal of self-confidence and not let herself be too intimidated by her male colleagues." She is motivated by the pleasure of success. "Success to me means that by doing good work, I get new and interesting assignments again and again."

She still finds something new to learn about her profession. "Each assignment is a completely new task for me. I find it easy to make drafts, but difficult to finalize them so that the continuity is always granted. This is the reason why I do all the artwork myself." She enjoys poster work the most. Because different sections of Switzerland speak different languages, Swiss projects are usually printed in German, Italian and French. Conversationally, Tissi favors German.

Portfolio of posters given as a promotional gift by Reprotechnik Koten AG, a printer.

ROSMARIE TISSI

"Formal education is helpful, but not important in all cases," Tissi, who was educated in Zurich, believes. She preferred studying geography and chemistry while growing up, and discovered art later. Geography was one impetus for her global roaming. "I am inspired by everyday life. Ideas come up suddenly. It is difficult to list what comes first in the design process. I think I am usually concentrating on everything at once — color, typography, form, composition."

Tissi feels that, at the moment, the design industry is not making much progress. She attributes that to too many unskilled people using the computer who have simply bought the equipment and are unsure how to produce good design with it. "Excellent graphic design is no longer possible if too much computer technique is involved. Some designers do not seem to have a style of their own any longer. What they produce is often boring and uninteresting. Many of them do not understand the basic rules of design because they haven't gotten proper schooling."

None of us is on earth for himself alone, each of us is here for all the others too

Human rights poster for "Artis 89."

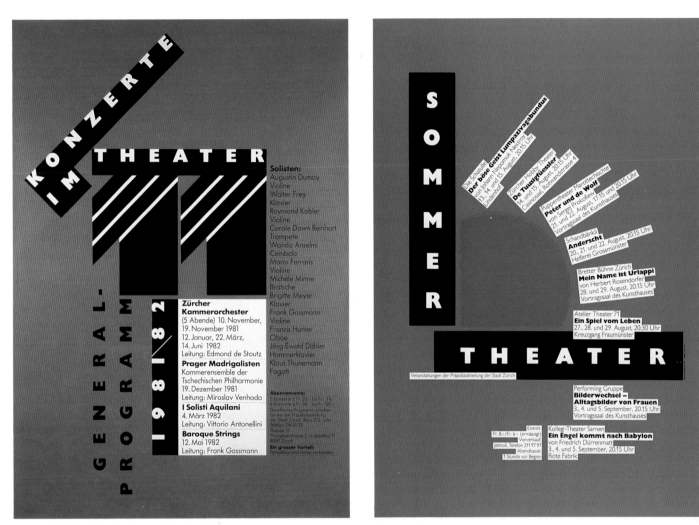

Program poster, introducing new logo, for Theater 11.

Summer theater poster.

One of a series of banknote designs.

ROSMARIE TISSI

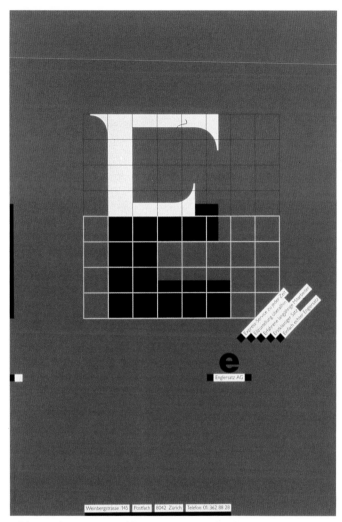

Ad for Englercomputergrafik, a computer graphics firm.

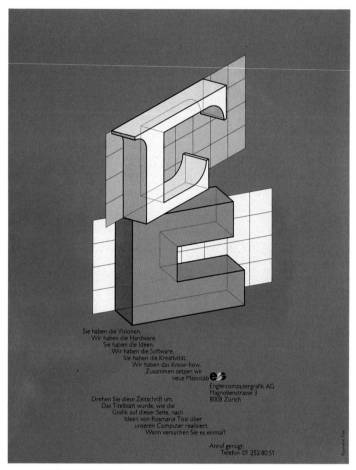

Poster for Englersatz AG, typesetters.

Water wheel logo
for a flour mill.

Poster for a series of concerts in the park.

Things have changed in the world since Tissi started her travels. The infrastructure of many exotic countries has become so unstable that much travel is dangerous. But there are still many places Tissi plans to see. She loves Zurich, but considers living in the Swiss countryside someday, on a farm with cats and a variety of other animals. "I don't know if that will ever really happen, but I will always have dreams. Or perhaps I will spend my extra money on another journey to a new land."

LYNN TRICKETT

Trickett + Webb
London, England

Lynn Trickett is an
introspective woman. "I am a
designer," she states, "every
minute of every day. It's
sometimes inconvenient,
because it means that I care
about things that other people
might not waste their time on
—" But she can also be
articulate and amusing.
" — like finding a tin opener
which not only works well,
but looks good. Not easy!"

Mail order catalogs for
Alphabet Soup,
an antiques dealer.

*"Lifestyle" brochure for Dorma,
a bed linens company.*

One of three partners of Trickett and Webb, we found her to be quite humble, too. "My success is a shared success," she'll tell you. "I've been very lucky in my choice of partners. My husband, Terry, is an architect and my partner, Brian Webb, is a graphic designer. Brian and I set up Trickett & Webb 21 years ago, having known each other for five weeks!" She laughs. "We always said that had we known each other better, we would never have risked it!"

Trickett's studio gets its work by recommendation or reputation, so every job that leaves the office has a role to play as a good ambassador. "At the end of the day," says Trickett, "our success depends upon the latest job we have produced. It's a mistake to underestimate your audience, so I try to squeeze a little wit and audience participation into our projects."

*Series of stamps entitled
"Memories" for Royal Mail.*

LYNN TRICKETT

She considers her strengths: "I think I have good ideas and a good eye." Essential characteristics when running a design group. "I think I'm quite good at recognizing people's strengths and making the most of them. It is important to me that Trickett & Webb functions well as a group of people — not just a work machine. We share our triumphs as well as our anxieties."

"On a personal level, I hope I'm a pretty good mother to my three kids," Trickett says. But "any working mother has to go through the guilt of always being at the wrong place at the wrong time. I've been very lucky to have a supportive husband, a great nanny and, of course, incredible children." Trickett also spends time with design students. "I act as an external assessor for art colleges. I am happiest spending time on student projects because I feel that I not only have something to give them, but I can learn, too. I advise new graduates to always aim high to begin with. You can always lower your sights, but it is harder to raise them."

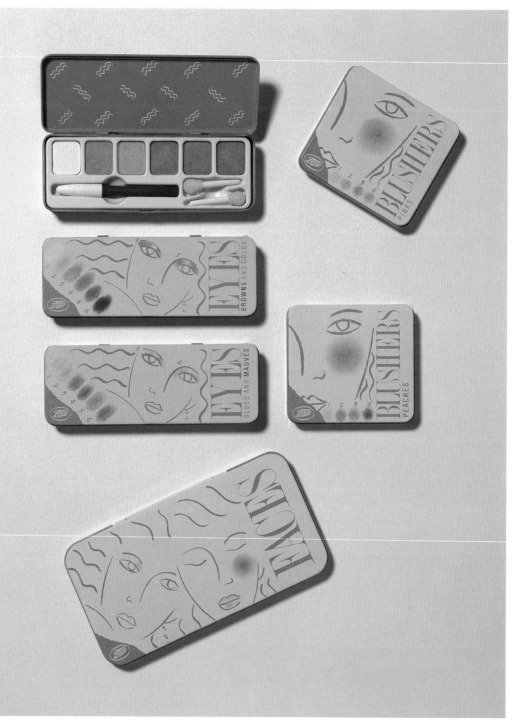

Identity for a line of cosmetics for young girls.

Packaging for a line of children's felt-tipped pens for WH Smith Ltd.

Packaging for "Creative Play," a series of activities for children.

Trickett originally wanted to be a sculptor. "Luckily for me," she laughs, "the head of the school didn't approve of women students. He said they weren't physically strong enough!" Instead, she joined a friend who had enrolled in a graphics class. "I'll always remember the first day, being totally boggled by type 'with bits on' and 'without' — my introduction to serif and sans serif typefaces."

LYNN TRICKETT

"Green Issue," a series of environmental stamps using children's winning illustrations.

But she had unknowingly joined a dynamic course headed by Edward Wright, whom she calls a "concrete poet." "He believed not only in typography, but was committed to ideas. He brought together a talented group of tutors and topped them up with incredible visiting lecturers like Robert Brownjohn and Bob Gill. This inspired me to visit New York, where I worked for a year or so. It was a wonderful, exciting place to be and gave me the confidence to bring the same values to my work when I returned to England."

A Royal Mail Christmas book titled Lickety Stick.

The Shoeshine Outfit,
a line of Christmas
gifts for men.

"I Am a Doughnut" calendar for screen printers, designers, and illustrators.

LYNN TRICKETT

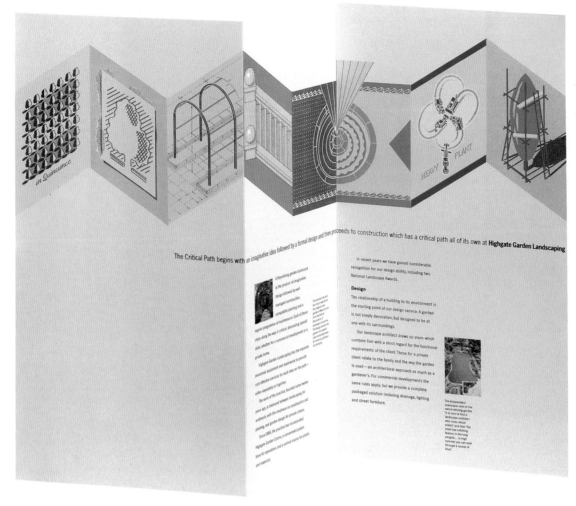

A *how-to-landscape brochure for Highgate Garden Centre.*

"The design process always starts with a steep learning curve," Trickett maintains. "I gather as much peripheral information as possible to think 'round the problem. It sounds corny, but I do find that many of my best ideas surface just before going to sleep. Then comes the hard part — getting the concept to communicate and look good, too. Part of my job at the studio is to know which designer's shoulder I should be looking over, based on their special skills. Some jobs stand or fall on immaculately detailed typography, whereas others are such strong ideas that the type must not be too obtrusive."

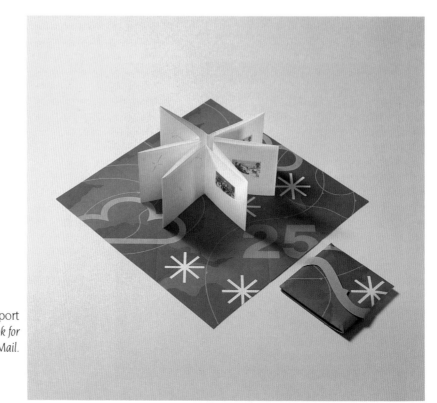

Weather Report *Christmas book for Royal Mail.*

Calendar for photographer Robert Dowling.

"Idea-based design is very important to me. I try to keep an open mind and open eyes to everything around me. I collect many different kinds of ephemera, art and books with a particular emphasis on the 1930s, 40s and 50s. I think you have to grab an idea from the side, catching it unawares. That way you end up with something unique and unpredictable."

Expressions, a line of recycled writing paper for WH Smith Ltd.

SUSANNA VALLEBONA

Esseblu
Milan, Italy

"**M**y ambition is to create a universal design message — a 'polyglot' image — at some point in my career," says Susanna Vallebona. "My work is very simple and easily assimilated, characteristics not always obvious to the viewer." Perhaps those are the elements that define my intention and my style."

Signage for S.O.S. Infanzia, an organization to assist abused children.

Book covers for
Elio Sellino Editore.

Poster for Tecnavia,
photo transmission technology.

Vallebona will tell you that she has very high standards, which makes her demanding and difficult to please. But we found her personable, enthusiastic about her work and quite sure of herself and her direction. "My use of line and color has been called 'consistent.' The message of my work comes from a combination of rigor, simplicity, surprise and show. I think I somewhat imitate Paul Klee's philosophy, 'I love the rule that proves feelings.' For me, I really love the feeling that proves the rule. Above all, I believe in the love of what I do."

SUSANNA VALLEBONA

Vallebona does not believe the creation of commercial art is "difficult" or "easy" — that some things are much more challenging and some are not. Instead, she is convinced that confusion arises when vision and purpose are muddled between designer and client. Clear up communications, she insists, and many of the problems of design would be eliminated.

She finds pleasure in the development of a plan. "The finished product gives me as much satisfaction as the idea when it begins to take shape," Vallebona says. "Usually, soon after the consulting stage, something starts moving and growing inside me. Ideas come from all directions, from elaboration on the original thought or from analysis. Sometimes they come on their own. Usually, you must seek them out."

Corporate identity
for publisher
Elio Sellino Editore.

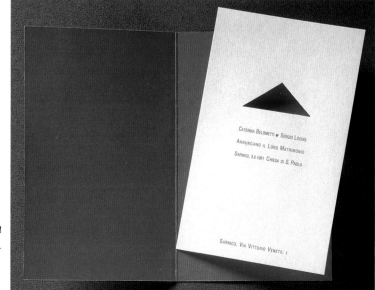

Wedding invitation
for Sergio Lochis.

Labels for a line of flavored vodkas by Lazza.

Label for Lazza amaretto liqueur.

SUSANNA VALLEBONA

"I am dedicated to this work because I have a passion for it," she says. "I define 'work' as meeting two different and often opposite requirements in graphics — the interests of the client and your own intention. In the Renaissance, for example, every artist had a very definite scheme to follow in his work — everything was defined in his contract and his clients even indicated the quantity and quality of the colors he should employ. Each work, nevertheless, expressed the artist's own personal feeling. There is no depiction of the 'Annunciation' that looks exactly like another."

When she was six years old, Vallebona remembers imagining herself older, doing the kind of work where you would create beautiful things using pens and pencils and colors. "I took all the planning and design courses that were offered in school. My favorite class of all was art history." Today, Vallebona thinks the industry is generally influenced by the United States, Japan and England. "I think the U.S. has much to teach about computers. The style of Japan and all the eastern industrialized countries attracts me for its feeling behind the trademark, and for its variety of

Event logo and brochure for a golf meeting sponsored by S.T. Dupont.

Trademark for Consulting Milano,
a building company.

Arcana Editrice logo
for a series of books with CD's.

SE E' SUCCESSO QUALCOSA
che ti
impedisce
di dormire,
telefonaci

SOS INFANZIA 091-443333/34

SE E' SUCCESSO QUALCOSA
di cui
non sai con chi
parlare,
telefonaci

SOS INFANZIA 091-443333/34

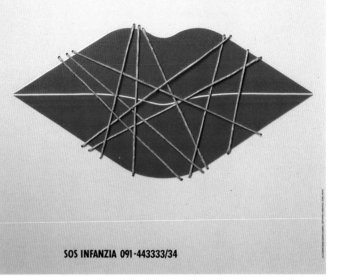

Ad campaign for S.O.S. Infanzia, an organization to assist abused children.

Giraffa Trading, a magazine for boys by producers of toys.

traditional, polished-style packaging. As far as Europe is concerned, I think the English school of graphic arts is still very much alive and valued. The Spanish and Dutch schools are close behind."

"I appreciate the freshness of the Barcelona school," Vallebona notes. But she gives some thought to the graphic environment in her own country. "The Italian school was very important up to the 1980s. At present, although Italian style is still much appreciated and respected, I think a change is necessary, particularly for young people, who need more room and challenge."

SUSANNA VALLEBONA

Promotional poster for
"Meie Assicurazioni,"
an annual celebration.

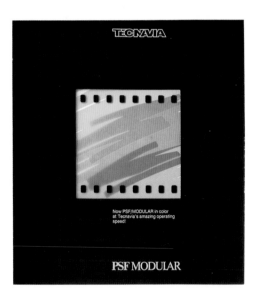

Brochure for Tecnavia, photo transmission technology.

SAVE ME
TO SAVE
YOURSELF

Poster for "Centro S. Fedele" competition.

With two children who occupy a majority of her free time, Vallebona spends many evenings at a favorite pastime — making up little nursery rhymes when it's time to put them to bed. "My husband teases me," she laughs, "and tells me I could have a chance as a very good babysitter if I fail as a graphic designer."

Vallebona recently invested in a computer, and she still enjoys talking about the new capabilities she has learned. "I am really charmed by the chances it gives me to create new pictures," she says. "It's just like having more power. And if technology offers a better way to realize one's own creativity, why not?"

NANCY WILLIAMS

Williams and Phoa
London, England

No frills — it's a method of design that's difficult to do well. But it has earned Nancy Williams a respected name with England's business community. "We cut back to basics," she says with the confidence of someone who has taken a risk and come out on the winning side. "There's no unnecessary decoration."

Annual report and accounts for Post Office Counters.

Looseleaf brochure for Paternoster Square development project.

Portfolio containing limited-edition horticultural prints presented at the opening of the Chelsea Flower Show.

Williams has designed everything from newspapers to book jackets to labels for wine and cheese. Then she founded the partnership of Williams and Phoa in 1984. "Our two styles complement each other," she asserts. "Our clients come to us not for a distinctive style, but because we can solve their problems. We want our work to be aesthetically pleasing, but business-oriented at the same time."

NANCY WILLIAMS

"With our design, everything that's on the page is necessary," Williams says. "It offers a certain purity about our work: a cleanness, a spareness. It's the common thread that makes our work different. It's not as much a look as an impression you get. We avoid fashion trends in graphics. If the trend is, for example, putting linear boxes around everything, we'll do that only if it serves a critical design function. We have uncompromising standards. We try lots of approaches to start, and only concentrate on one idea, so that the message is as clear as possible."

Prospectus for Inchbald School of Design.

Stationery for Nicholas Gill Associates, architects.

Williams explored art, especially painting, while she was growing up, but didn't have enough confidence to pursue art school at first. It was an art teacher who encouraged her to go. "Art school was like coming home," she said. "I got on with everyone. Before art school, I was so hopeless. Everything creative was slightly frowned on in the school I had been attending. In fact, when I was a teenager, design was something I didn't even know existed."

NANCY WILLIAMS

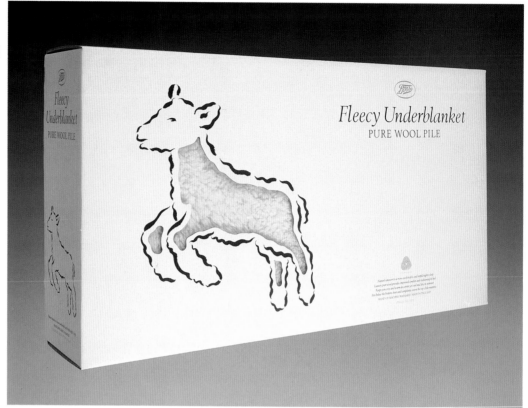

Packaging for a wool blanket by Boots.

Her favorite part of the graphics process is the detailing, and she excels at it. "I can get the type to work beautifully with the text. I enjoy getting the balance of color right." Williams ends her design process with color application. "I believe everything should first work in black and white," she notes.

"Other countries and cultures are a great source of inspiration for my work," says Williams. She can often distinguish the traits in design that identify its cultural source. "If it's from America, you can see that; if it's from Britain, you can see that, too. British work is usually not as slick as American work. Japanese design often has very clean lines, and ranges from frenetic to elegant and stylish."

Book design for Ehrets Flowering Plants.

Brochure for Roughton and Fenton, engineers.

Project brochure for Olympia & York's Canary Wharf development.

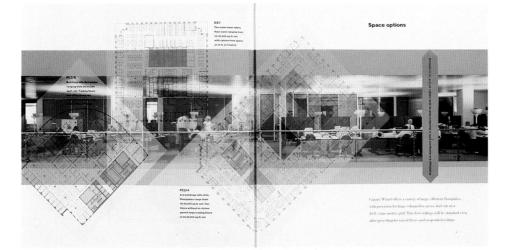

Williams has come a long way in bridging the communications gulf between designers and clients, but she feels she's not quite there yet. "Many clients see design as the means to an end, and don't appreciate its value. They may wish to use a certain photographer because of his or her quality of work, but they use another because their first choice is too expensive. We hope eventually clients will become more educated about design and be willing to spend the appropriate funds on projects so we, as designers, can produce the best work available."

NANCY WILLIAMS

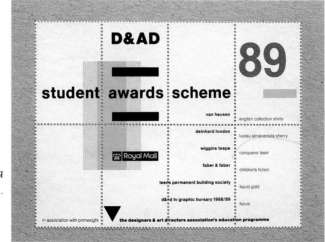

Brochure for TTSP, architects.

She feels some designers have become complacent about their work. "The design industry got a terrible name in the 1980s because of the greed of a few. The recession was healthy in that respect because some of these firms that were in business solely to make as much money as possible did not survive. We still see careless work and are appalled that people have paid their hard-earned money for it. Designers in powerful positions should take their work seriously. All of us need to know the business and serve the customer ethically."

Call for entries for a student awards competition.

Outside the studio, few can match Williams' enthusiasm for creating culinary masterpieces. "I love to cook anything, though there's very little time for that these days." Most of her preferred recipes are Italian. "Cooking relaxes me," says Williams, who, as a young adult, entertained the idea of becoming a chef.

Williams, who employs a staff of 16 people at Williams and Phoa, will tell you she doesn't work well in isolation. "I have an idyllic dream of a cottage in the country where I can someday achieve creative fulfillment without stress. But I need a lot of people around me. So maybe Florence each summer would suffice."

Wine labels for France Vin Limited.

Corporate brochure for Extel.

Credits

MADELEINE BENNETT

PAGE 2

Packaging and advertisement for Giorgio Armani eyewear.
Art Director and Designer: Madeleine Bennett
Design Firm: Michael Peters & Partners

PAGE 3

Packaging and logo application for Penhaligon's, a perfumerie.
Art Director and Designer: Madeleine Bennett
Design Firm: Michael Peters & Partners

PAGE 4

Brand identity and packaging for Classicus pens, Plus Corporation.
Art Director and Designer: Madeleine Bennett
Design Firm: Michael Peters & Partners

Packaging for Free & Free, a brand of hair care products by Lion Corporation.
Art Director and Designer: Madeleine Bennett
Design Consultant: Michael Peters (Asia Pacific)
Bottle Constructor: Product First

PAGE 5

Brochure and identity for International Coffee Organisation, trade association.
Art Director and Designer: Madeleine Bennett
Design Firm: Michael Peters & Partners

Label design for a line of gourmet preserves by Elsenham Foods.
Art Director and Designer: Madeleine Bennett
Design Firm: Michael Peters & Partners

PAGE 6

Identity and related packaging for The British Museum Shop.
Art director and Designer: Madeleine Bennett
Design Firm: Michael Peters & Partners
Client: British Museum Publications

Packaging for the fragrances of Joseph, Parfum de Jour.
Art Director and Designer: Madeleine Bennett
Design Firm: Michael Peters & Partners

PAGE 7

Identity for Body Bar, a chocolate snack aimed at young, health-conscious Japanese men.
Art Director and Designer: Madeleine Bennett
Design Firm: Michael Peters & Partners
Client: Meiji Seika

PAGE 8 & 9

Several of 28 posters for the 1992 Olympic Games in Barcelona, Spain.
Art Director and Designer: Madeleine Bennett
Design Firm: Michael Peters & Partners
Client: COOB '92 SA (Comité Organizador Olímpico Barcelona '92)
Photographers: NASA, Allsport, Kishimoto, Firo Photo

BETHANY BUNNELL

PAGE 10

Portrait Photographer: Ringo Tang

Invitation and announcement for Bunnell's wedding.
Art Director and Designer: Bethany Bunnell
Design Firm: Bunnell Design
Client: Bunnell and Schmidt

PAGE 11

One of a series of MTV in Asia posters done to promote the five STAR TV channels.
Art Directors: Bethany Bunnell and Joe Kurzer
Designer: Catherine Lam Siu-hung
Design Firm: STAR TV Creative Services
Client: STAR TV

PAGE 12

Bamboo logo for MTV in Asia.
Art Directors: Bethany Bunnell and Joe Kurzer
Designer and Illustrator: Bethany Bunnell
Design Firm: STAR TV Creative Services (Original MTV logo designed by Manhattan Design)
Client: STAR TV

Levis/MTV limited-edition jeans jacket.
Art Directors and Designers: Bethany Bunnell and Joe Kurzer
Design Firm: STAR TV Creative Services
Client: STAR TV

PAGE 13

Press kit for MTV.
Art Director: Bethany Bunnell
Designers: Bethany Bunnell and Catherine Lam Siu-hung
Design Firm: STAR TV Creative Services
Client: STAR TV

Invitation for the 1992 MTV Video Music Awards.
Art Director: Jeff Keyton (MTV, New York)
Designer: Bethany Bunnell
Design Firm: STAR TV Creative Services
Client: STAR TV

PAGE 14

Identity and stationery for STAR TV.
Art Directors and Designers: Bethany Bunnell and Joe Kurzer
Design Firm: STAR TV Creative Services

Event banners for STAR TV Laser Show, organized to promote AIDS awareness.
Art Directors: Bethany Bunnell and Joe Kurzer
Designers: Bethany Bunnell, Joe Kurzer, and Sharon Battat
Design Firms: STAR TV Creative Services and ArtHouse
Client: STAR TV

PAGE 15

Tickets, program, and sweatshirt.
Art Directors and Designers: Bethany Bunnell and Joe Kurzer
Design Firm: STAR TV Creative Services
Client: STAR TV

Event graphics.
Art Directors and Designers: Bethany Bunnell and Joe Kurzer
Design Firm: STAR TV Creative Services
Client: STAR TV

PAGE 16

Corporate identity and stationery for The Tomson Group, property developer and investor.
Art Director and Designer: Bethany Bunnell
Design Firm: Bunnell Design

PAGE 17

Logo and letterhead for Sun Moon Star Corporation.
Art Director: Leila Nachtigall
Designer: Bethany Bunnell
Design Firm: Landor Associates

Identity manual for Sun Moon Star Corporation.
Art Director: Leila Nachtigall
Designer: Bethany Bunnell
Design Firm: Landor Associates

MARGO CHASE

PAGE 18

Video disk sleeve for jazz drummer Tony Williams.
Art Director and Designer: Margo Chase
Designer and Calligrapher: Nancy Ogami
Photographer: Margo Chase
Client: Blue Note Records

PAGE 19

Poster for Gelinas, maker of salon hair care products.
Art Director: Margo Chase
Designers: Margo Chase and Lorna Stovall
Photographer: Mindas
Client: Triune Research, Inc.

PAGE 20

Layout for article on experimental typography and design.
Designer: Margo Chase
Clients: Semiotext(e) Magazine and Hraztan Zeitlian

Packaging for Santa Cruz blue corn tortilla chips.
Designer: Margo Chase
Client: R.W. Garcia

PAGE 21

Logo for Madonna's "Like a Prayer" album.
Art Director: Jeri Heiden, Warner Bros. Records
Designer: Margo Chase
Client: Warner Bros. Records

Logo for "The Voices," a hard rock band.
Designer: Margo Chase
Client: MCA Records

PAGE 22

CD packaging for Cher's "Love Hurts" album.
Designer and Illustrator: Margo Chase
Photographers: Herb Ritts and Merlin Rosenberg
Client: Geffen Records

Generic sleeve for Virgin Records.
Art Director: Melanie Nissen, Virgin Records
Designers: Margo Chase and Alan Disparte

PAGE 23

Stationery for Margo Chase Design.
Art Director and Designer: Margo Chase

"This Could Be Such a Beautiful World,"
promotional T-shirt design.
Designer: Margo Chase

PAGE 24

Promotional poster, entitled "Germs,"
for Chase's speaking engagement.
Designer: Margo Chase
Client: Albert College of Art

"Renaissance" album packaging.
Art Director: Kim Champain, Warner Bros. Records
Designer: Margo Chase
Photographer: Sidney Cooper

Comprehensive for Virgin Records'
generic sleeve.
Art Director: Melanie Nissen, Virgin Records
Designer: Margo Chase

SHEILA LEVRANT
DE BRETTEVILLE

PAGE 26

Book cover and interior spread of *The*
Motown Album.
Art Director and Designer: Sheila Levrant
de Bretteville
Studio Assistants: Jennifer Egger and Vivian Chow
Editor: Marianne Partridge
Clients: St. Martin's Press, The Berry Gordy
Company, and Sarah Lazin Books

PAGE 27

Catalog cover and interior spread for
an exhibition of "The Art of Betye and
Alison Saar."
Art Director and Designer: Sheila Levrant
de Bretteville
Studio Assistants: Jennifer Egger and Vivian Chow
Client: Wright Gallery, University of California at
Los Angeles

PAGE 28 & 29

Five different views of an 8' x 82' mural
depicting life and contributions of Biddy
Mason, midwife and former slave.
Art Director and Designer: Sheila Levrant
de Bretteville
Studio Assistant: Jennifer Egger
Photographer: Julie Eaton
Clients: The Community Redevelopment Agency of
Los Angeles, Power of Place, and the African
American Communities of Los Angeles

PAGE 30

Poster for the "Architecture and Design
Film Festival."
Art Director and Designer: Sheila Levrant
de Bretteville
Photographer: Ave Pildas
Airbrush artist: Charles Calvo
Printer: Alan Lithograph

PAGE 31

Logo sculpture for CBS Cable, a short-lived
fine arts channel.
Art Director and Designer: Sheila Levrant
de Bretteville
Studio Assistant: Jerry Kuyper

PAGE 32

Letterhead, pouch box, and video box for
Warner Bros. Records.
Art Director and Designer: Sheila Levrant
de Bretteville
Studio Assistant: Vivian Chow
Clients: John Beug and Jeri Heiden, Warner
Bros. Records

PAGE 33

Invitation for "High Tea in Hollywood," the
opening of a new public library designed
by Frank Gehry.
Art Director and Designer: Sheila Levrant
de Bretteville
Printer: Franklin Press

Betye Saar, art catalog.
Art Director and Designer: Sheila Levrant
de Bretteville
Clients: Museum of Contemporary Art and Betye Saar
Printer: Typecraft

ANNA EYMONT

PAGE 34

"Water," a presentation folder on
wastewater reuse.
Art Director: Anna Eymont
Designer: Sharon Pearson
Client: Gutteridge Haskins & Davey, Consulting
Engineers

PAGE 35

Logo, menus, and stationery for Bobbin Inn.
Art Director: Anna Eymont
Designers: Alison Hulett and Myriam Kin-Yee

Community education logo for the
Waterboard of New South Wales.
Art Director: Myriam Kin-Yee
Designer: Frank Chin

PAGE 36

Exhibition panels for the National Australian
Maritime Museum.
Art Director: Anna Eymont
Designer: Myriam Kin-Yee

Posters for the National Australian Maritime
Museum.
Art Director: Anna Eymont
Designer: Myriam Kin-Yee

PAGE 37

Brochure for the Australian Human Rights
and Equal Opportunity Commission.
Art Director: Myriam Kin-Yee
Designer: Sharon Pearson

PAGE 38

Promotional material for Lincoln Downs,
a country resort.
Designer: Alison Hulett

Presentation folder and brochure for GHD
International.
Art Director: Anna Eymont
Designer: Frank Chin

PAGE 39

Poster and brochures for the Affirmative
Action Agency.
Art Director: Myriam Kin-Yee
Designer: Sharon Pearson

PAGE 40

Annual report for OPSM Industries Limited.
Art Director: Anna Eymont
Designer: Eden Cartwright

"Movies at the Metcalfe" poster for the State
Library of New South Wales.
Art Director: Anna Eymont
Designer: Myriam Kin-Yee

PAGE 41

Menus for Bayswater Brasserie.
Designer: Alison Hulett

Logo and bottle label for Australian
Spring Water.
Art Director: Alison Hulett
Designer: Frank Chin

APRIL GREIMAN

PAGE 42

Cover of *Hybrid Imagery: The Fusion of*
Technology and Graphic Design, book featuring
work of April Greiman, Inc.
Art Director and Designer: April Greiman

PAGE 43

Poster for Southern California Institute of
Architecture.
Art Director and Designer: April Greiman
Design Associate: Sean Adams

PAGE 44

Summer program book for Southern
California Institute of Architecture.
Art Director and Designer: April Greiman
Design Associate: Sean Adams

Invitational poster for Sir Jack Zunz.
Art Director and Designer: April Greiman
Client: Ove Arup & Partners

PAGE 45

Poster for summer sessions of the University
of California at Los Angeles.
Art Director and Designer: April Greiman

PAGE 46

Woven textile for "Harlequin."
Art Director and Designer: April Greiman
Design Associate: Noreen Morioka
Client: Cerritos Center for the Performing Arts

Stationery for Cerritos Center for the Performing Arts.
Art Director and Designer: April Greiman

Tile motifs for Cerritos Center for the Performing Arts.
Art Director and Designer: April Greiman
Architect: Barton Myers Associates

PAGE 47

"Vitra Neocon," a fold-out poster for Vitra Seating, Inc., chair manufacturer.
Art Director and Designer: April Greiman
Design Associate: Sean Adams

PAGE 48

Poster and billboard for "Graphic Design in America," an exhibit of the Walker Art Center.
Art Director and Designer: April Greiman

Poster for the Museum of Modern Art's exhibit, "The Modern Poster."
Art Director and Designer: April Greiman

PAGE 49

Stationery system for Roto NDI Architects.
Art Director and Designer: April Greiman

Restaurant signage for China Club.
Art Director and Designer: April Greiman

CATHERINE HAUGHTON

PAGE 50

Newsletter for a Ford of Canada car dealer.
Art Directors: Catherine Haughton and Philip Brazeau
Designer: David Thorne
Illustrators: Various

PAGE 51

Circus characters featured on stationery for Haughton Brazeau.
Art Directors: Catherine Haughton and Philip Brazeau
Designers: Haughton Brazeau staff
Illustrator: John Craig

Promotional items for the "Second Annual Haughton Brazeau Air Show & Family Picnic," a thank-you for clients, staff, and suppliers.
Art Directors: Catherine Haughton and Philip Brazeau
Designer: Sandra King
Illustrator: Nancy Stahl

PAGE 52

Self-promotion, entitled "Winning Combinations."
Art Director: Catherine Haughton
Designer: Derwyn Goodall
Photographer: Peter Horvath

PAGE 53

Identity for Anderson Public Relations.
Art Director: Catherine Haughton
Designer: Bob Wheller

Unifying symbol for NewTel Enterprises Ltd.
Art Directors: Catherine Haughton and Philip Brazeau
Designer: Derwyn Goodall

Annual report for NewTel Enterprises Ltd.
Art Directors: Catherine Haughton and Philip Brazeau
Designer: Derwyn Goodall
Illustrator: Tomio Nitto

PAGE 54

Stationery for photographer Barbara Cole.
Art Director: Catherine Haughton
Designer, Illustrator, and Typographer: James Forrester

Annual report for Household Finance Corporation.
Art Director: Catherine Haughton
Designer: James Forrester
Photographer: Barbara Cole

PAGE 55

Ontario Hydro's diverse market is depicted in its annual report.
Art Directors: Catherine Haughton and Philip Brazeau
Designer: Derwyn Goodall
Photographer: Paul Orenstien

Annual report for Markborough Properties.
Art Director: Catherine Haughton
Designer: Derwyn Goodall
Photographers: Various

PAGE 56

Annual report for World Wildlife Fund Canada.
Art Directors: Catherine Haughton and Philip Brazeau
Designer: Derwyn Goodall
Illustrator: Jacobson Fernandes

PAGE 57

Corporate brochure for Wood Gundy, international investors.
Art Director: Catherine Haughton
Designer: Derwyn Goodall
Photographer: Ed Gadjel

JANE HOPE

PAGE 58

Bar coaster for Smirnoff Vodka, "*Rouge comme l'enfer*" (Red hot).
Art Director and Designer: Jane Hope
Illustrator: Alain Pilon

PAGE 59

Promotional packaging for Maple Leaf Tea.
Art Director, Designer, and Copywriter: Jane Hope
Illustrator: Nina Berkson

PAGE 60

Poster for "L'*art dans la rue*" (Art in the Street), a City of Montreal event.
Art Director, Designer, Illustrator, and Copywriter: Jane Hope

PAGE 61

Stationery for Alfafa, advertising agency.
Art Director and Designer: Jane Hope

Packaging for CCM Inlines Skates.
Art Director, Designer, and Illustrator: Jane Hope

PAGE 62

Poster and postcard for architectural conference, "Montreal 1990."
Art Director and Designer: Jane Hope
Illustrator: Daniel Sylvestre

PAGE 63

Billboards for McDonald's, "*Je ne peux pas y résister*" (I can't resist).
Art Director and Designer: Jane Hope
Copywriter: Jacques Labelle
Photographers: Michel Pilon and Adrien Duey

PAGE 64

Campaign logo for Tireurs d'élite (Sharpshooters), media service professionals.
Art Director and Designer: Jane Hope
Copywriter: Martin Gosselin

Poster for "Foster Horse Show."
Art Director, Designer, and Illustrator: Jane Hope

PAGE 65

Stationery for Lynn Paradis, psychologist.
Art Director and Designer: Jane Hope

Poster for Biodôme, the living museum.
Art Director and Designer: Jane Hope
Illustrators: Helmut Langeder, Christian Hupfer, and Mario Berthiaume
Copywriter: Martin-Éric Ouellette

DITI KATONA

PAGE 66

"Printed in Canada" brochure and press kit for the Canadian Printing Industries Association.
Art Directors: John Pylypczak and Diti Katona
Designers: John Pylypczak and Susan MacIntee

PAGE 67

Stationery for Concrete Design Communications Inc.
Art Directors and Designers: Diti Katona and John Pylypczak
Illustrator: Ross MacDonald

Moving announcement for Concrete Design.
Art Directors and Designers: Diti Katona and John Pylypczak
Illustrator: Ross MacDonald

PAGE 68

Brochure introducing Zapata's line of designer clothing.
Art Director and Designer: Diti Katona
Photographer: Deborah Samuel

Brochure introducing Zapata's line of spring 1993 clothing.
Art Director: Diti Katona
Designers: Diti Katona and John Pylypczak
Calligrapher: John Pylypczak

PAGE 69

Cover and inside spread of an employee annual report.
Art Directors and Designers: John Pylypczak and Diti Katona
Illustrator: Jamie Bennet
Client: Noranda Inc.

PAGE 70

New products brochure for Keilhauer, a seating manufacturer.
Art Directors and Designers: Diti Katona and John Pylypczak
Illustrator: Mike Constable

Employee annual report for Noranda Inc., a natural resource company.
Art Director and Designer: Diti Katona
Designer: Victoria Primicias
Photographer: Chris Nicholls

PAGE 71

Stationery for DuVerre, a housewares retailer.
Art Director and Designer: Diti Katona
Photographer: Chris Nicholls

Self-promotional calendar for Concrete Design.
Art Directors and Designers: Diti Katona and John Pylypczak
Illustrator: Ross MacDonald

PAGE 72

Panorama, employee newsmagazine on the future of Canada.
Art Directors: Diti Katona and John Pylypczak
Designer: Victoria Primicias
Client: Noranda Inc.

PAGE 73

"Flexplan" benefits package for a natural resource company.
Art Directors and Designers: John Pylypczak and Diti Katona
Designer: John Pylypczak
Client: Noranda Inc.

Annual report for Northern Telecom.
Art Directors and Designers: John Pylypczak and Diti Katona
Illustrator: Doug Fraser

Annual report for First Mercantile Currency Fund.
Art Directors: Diti Katona and John Pylypczak
Designer: Diti Katona
Photographer: Ron Baxter Smith
Client: First Mercantile Corporation.

SIOBHAN KEANEY

PAGE 74

Poster for TDK videotapes.
Art Director: Geoff Southons
Designer, Typographer, and 3D Imager: Siobhan Keaney
Copywriter: Graham Pugh
Photographer: Robert Shackleton
Advertising Agency: Reay Keating Hamer

PAGE 75

Promotional materials for The Mill, a post-production company.
Art Director, Designer, and 3D Imager: Siobhan Keaney
Illustrators: Amelia Davies and Siobhan Keaney
Photographer: Robert Shackleton

PAGE 76

Stationery for The Mill.
Art Director, Designer, and 3D Imager: Siobhan Keaney
Illustrators: Amelia Davies and Siobhan Keaney
Photographer: Robert Shackleton

"Freedom" stamp for an exhibition at The Design Museum in London.
Art Director, Designer, and Photographer: Siobhan Keaney

Subscription promotion for EYE M*agazine*.
Art Director and Designer: Siobhan Keaney
Photographers: Robert Shackleton and Siobhan Keaney

PAGE 77

Poster for Seymour Powell, a product design company.
Art Director, Designer, and Illustrator: Siobhan Keaney

PAGE 78

Christmas accessories brochure for Browns, a high-fashion retailer.
Art Director and Designer: Siobhan Keaney
Photographer: Robert Shackleton

PAGE 79

Annual report for Apicorp, emphasizing the importance of nature and its resources.
Art Director, Designer, and 3D Imager: Siobhan Keaney
Photographers: Robert Shackleton and Siobhan Keaney

PAGE 80

Brochure and mailer for King Tilly, a design and advertising recruitment company.
Art Director, Designer, and 3D Imager: Siobhan Keaney
Photographers: Siobhan Keaney and Robert Shackleton

Typographic images for a Letraset catalog.
Art Director and Designer: Siobhan Keaney
Photographers: Robert Shackleton and Siobhan Keaney

PAGE 81

Brochure for Seymour Powell, commemorating the company's fifth year anniversary.
Art Director, Designer, and Illustrator: Siobhan Keaney

Stationery for Seymour Powell.
Art Director, Designer: Siobhan Keaney

JUDY KIRPICH

PAGE 82

Introductory brochure for the National Museum of the American Indian.
Art Directors and Designers: Judy F. Kirpich and Jim Jackson
Photographers: Walter Bigbee, Karen Furth, Randy Wells, and Taran Z
Printer: Virginia Lithograph

PAGE 83

Poster for "Systems Center 1989 User Conference."
Art Directors and Designers: Judy F. Kirpich and Richard Hamilton
Copywriter: John Temple
Photographer: Emily Medvec
Math Consultant: Aaron Kirpich
Printer: Virginia Lithograph

PAGE 84

"Wave of the Future" poster for VM Software.
Art Director and Designer: Judy F. Kirpich
Illustrator: Bradley Pomeroy, in part
Printer: Virginia Lithograph

Direct-mail promotion for Virginia Lithograph.
Art Directors and Designers: Judy F. Kirpich and Claire Wolfman
Illustrator: Liz Wolf
Copywriter: Roger Chavez
Printer: Virginia Lithograph

PAGE 85

Promotional box for Esse brand recycled paper.
Art Directors and Designers: Melanie Bass, Gregg Glaviano, and Judy F. Kirpich
Artist: Betsy Shields
Copywriter: Jake Pollard
Photographer: Claude Vasquez
Printer: Virginia Lithograph
Client: Gilbert Paper

PAGE 86

Museum catalog showcasing drawings and sketches of Josef Albers.
Art Directors and Designers: Judy F. Kirpich and Richard Hamilton
Printer: South China Press
Client: Art Services International

"Information Age" poster for the National Museum of American History.
Art Directors and Designers: Judy F. Kirpich, Gregg Glaviano, Melanie Bass, and Jennifer Johnson
Photographer: Joel Freid
Printer: Virginia Lithograph

PAGE 87

Senior citizens housing brochure for B'nai B'rith.
Art Director and Designer: Judy F. Kirpich

Annual report for Systems Center, Inc.
Art Directors and Designers: Judy F. Kirpich, Richard Hamilton, and Claire Wolfman
Illustrators: Andrzej Dudzinski, Lonnie Sue Johnson, John Howard, Vivienne Flesher, Skip Liepke, and Tom Curry
Copywriter: John Temple
Printer: Virginia Lithograph

PAGE 88

Palindrome card deck for Graphik Communications.
Art Directors and Designers: Melanie Bass, Gregg Glaviano, Judy F. Kirpich, and Julie Sebastianelli
Illustrators: Bob James and Evangelia Philippidis
Copywriter: Jake Pollard
Printer: Virginia Lithograph

Virginia Lithograph "Book of Records."
Art Directors and Designers: Judy F. Kirpich,
Beth Bathe, and Claire Wolfman
Illustrator: Mercedes McDonald
Copywriter: Roger Chevez

PAGE 89

Poster for exhibit of Hollywood memorabilia.
Art Directors and Designers: Judy F. Kirpich and
Claire Wolfman
Illustrator: Doug Johnson
Printer: Virginia Lithograph
Client: Smithsonian Institution Traveling Exhibition
Service

SONSOLES LLORENS

PAGE 90

1991 Self-promotional New Year's cards.
Art Director and Designer: Sonsoles Llorens

PAGE 91

In-store tags for System Action clothing.
Art Director and Designer: Sonsoles Llorens

Spring catalog for System Action clothing.
Art Director and Designer: Sonsoles Llorens
Photographer: Galilea Nin

PAGE 92

Logo, letterhead, and shopping bag for
Arropa, a casual clothing store.
Art Director and Designer: Sonsoles Llorens

PAGE 93

Poster for "Exposició i Activitats Noves
Imatges," an exhibit of graphic, holographic,
and computer art.
Art Director and Designer: Sonsoles Llorens

PAGE 94

Invitation to "Bulevart," a cocktail reception
and art exhibit for Bulevard Rosa shopping
center's third anniversary.
Art Director and Designer: Sonsoles Llorens
Photographer: Ferrán Freiza

Identity applications for Mon Bar (World
Bar), a beer and *tapas* pub.
Art Director and Designer: Sonsoles Llorens

PAGE 95

Stationery and signage for Biennale des
Jeunes Créateurs d'Europe de la
Méditerranée.
Art Director and Designer: Sonsoles Llorens

PAGE 96

Letterhead and brochure for Tenispaña, the
commercial division of the Royal Spanish
Tennis Federation.
Art Director and Designer: Sonsoles Llorens
Photographer: Pep Ávila

PAGE 97

Poster and T-shirt promoting the Spain vs.
Israel Davis Cup elimination round.
Art Director and Designer: Sonsoles Llorens

NORA OLGYAY

PAGE 98

Promotional brochure for ANA's (All Nippan
Airways) Pacific Bonus Program.
Art Director: Nora Olgyay
Designers: Nora Olgyay and Laurie Swindull
Copywriter: Hakuhodo, Inc.
Photographer: Oi Veerasarn
Typographer: Composition Services, Inc.
Printer: Virginia Lithograph

PAGE 99

Identity, stationery, and collateral pieces for
Thai-One-On, a Thai food caterer.
Art Director and Designer: Nora Olgyay
Photographer: Oi Veerasarn
Typographer: Phil's Photo & Composition Services, Inc.
Printer: River Press, Inc.

PAGE 100

Stationery, announcement, and marketing
materials for LeMay Associates, an
architectural firm.
Art Director: Nora Olgyay
Designers: Nora Olgyay, Jean Steele, and Tony Hines
Photographer: Oi Veerasarn
Typographer: Composition Services, Inc.
Printer: Westland Printers

Marketing, fund-raising, and membership
materials for the National Building Museum.
Art Director: Nora Olgyay
Designers: Nora Olgyay and James Doussard
Photographer: Oi Veerasarn
Typographer: Composition Services, Inc.
Printer: Minuteman Press

PAGE 101

"Creating the Southeast Federal Center," a
condensation of a formal, five-volume
government development proposal.
Art Director: Nora Olgyay
Designers: Nora Olgyay and Supon Phornirunlit,
Supon Design Group, Inc.
Photographer: Oi Veerasarn
Typographer: Composition Services, Inc.
Printer: S&S Graphics, Inc.
Client: Federal Center Associates, Inc.

Design and implementation of the
environmental graphics of London's Canary
Wharf development.
Art Director: Nora Olgyay
Designers: Nora Olgyay, John Branigan, Edwin
Schlossberg, Inc., and Various
Architects: I.M. Pei Associates; Cesar Pelli &
Associates; Skidmore, Owings & Merrill; Kohn,
Pedersen, Fox Associates; and Various
Photographer: Oi Veerasarn
Client: Olympia & York Developments, Inc.

PAGE 102

Signage standards program for one of BDM
Corporation's regional headquarters.
Art Director: Nora Olgyay
Designers: Nora Olgyay, Susan Bickford, and
James Doussard
Architect: Hellmuth, Obata & Kasabaum, Inc.
Fabricator: Cornelius Architectural Products
Copywriter: Nora Olgyay
Photographer: Oi Veerasarn

Architectural design criteria manual for retail
tenants of The Tysons II Galleria.
Art Director: Nora Olgyay
Designers: Nora Olgyay and James Doussard
Photographer: Oi Veerasarn
Typographer: Composition Services, Inc.
Printer: Virginia Lithograph
Client: Homart Development Co.

PAGE 103

Identity and architectural graphics for
Washington, D.C.'s Van Ness Station.
Art Director: Nora Olgyay
Designers: Nora Olgyay and Susan Bickford
Fabricator: Architectural Graphics, Inc.
Photographer: Oi Veerasarn
Client: The Lenkin Company Management, Inc.

Interior signage for a regional headquarters
of McGraw-Hill, Inc.
Art Director and Designer: Nora Olgyay
Architect: Spector, Knapp & Baughman, Ltd.
Fabricators: Cornelius Architectural Products and
Environmental Graphics Systems
Photographer: Larry Olsen

Fund-raising poster and tabletop display for
a soup kitchen.
Art Director and Designer: Nora Olgyay
Photographer: Oi Veerasarn
Client: The University Community Soup Kitchen

PAGE 104

Draft spread and sketches from the book
Safety Symbols: A National System.
Art Director: Nora Olgyay
Designers: Nora Olgyay and Sheila Woodbridge
Copywriter: Nora Olgyay
Photographer: Oi Veerasarn
Client: National Endowment for the Arts

Proposed information pylons for
Philadephia's 30th Street Train Station.
Art Director: Nora Olgyay
Designers: Nora Olgyay and Kelly O'Kane
Architect: Hellmuth, Obata & Kasabaum, Inc.
Photographer: Oi Veerasarn
Client: Gerald D. Hines Interests

PAGE 105

Standardized icons from the book *Safety*
Sumbols: A National System.
Art Director: Nora Olgyay
Designers: Nora Olgyay and Sheila Woodbridge
Copywriter: Nora Olgyay
Photographer: Oi Veerasarn
Client: National Endowment for the Arts

PAULA SCHER

PAGE 106

Packaging for nuts and popcorn for Oola
candy stores.
Art Director and Designer: Paula Scher

PAGE 107

Store front of Oola candy store.
Art Director and Designer: Paula Scher

Shopping bags for Oola candy stores.
Art Director and Designer: Paula Scher

PAGE 108

Poster for inaugural party of Bard College's Center for Curatorial Studies.
Art Director and Designer: Paula Scher

PAGE 109

Cover and spreads from "Useless Information," part of a promotional series for Champion International Corporation's Kromekote paper.
Creative Directors: Paula Scher and William Drentell, Drentell Doyle Partners
Art Director: Paula Scher
Copywriters: Paula Scher and Tony Hendra

PAGE 110

In-store display for UVU, a television set by RCA (Thompson Consumer Electronics).
Art Directors and Designers: Paula Scher and Ron Louie

Boxes as point-of-purchase display for UVU.
Art Directors and Designers: Paula Scher and Ron Louie

PAGE 111

Poster for Scher's speaking engagements in Tulsa and Oklahoma City, Oklahoma.
Art Director and Designer: Paula Scher

Cover for the 1992 Extension Catalog of the University of California at Los Angeles.
Art Director and Designer: Paula Scher

PAGE 112

Long box, CD, and booklet for Bob James and Earl Klugh, Warner Bros. Records.
Art Director and Designer: Paula Scher
Photographer: John Paul Endress

PAGE 113

Subway and bus shelter poster for the School of Visual Arts.
Art Director and Designer: Paula Scher

Cover for the 1991 *Annual of the American Institute of Graphic Arts.*
Art Director and Designer: Paula Scher

ELLEN SHAPIRO

PAGE 114

Portrait Photographer: Copyright 1992, Marion Goldman

Cover and spread of *Upper and Lower Case* (U&lc).
Art Director and Designer: Ellen Shapiro
Calligrapher: Donald Jackson

PAGE 115

Custom patient menus for Beth Israel Medical Center's Food and Nutrition Service.
Art Director and Designer: Ellen Shapiro
Painter: Susan Stillman

Development brochure for The Singers Forum, a vocal arts school and performance center.
Art Director and Designer: Ellen Shapiro
Illustrator of Eartha Kitt: Michael Witte
Cover Photographer: Christie Sherman

PAGE 116

Identity program, including annual report and "Op-Ed" advertising, for United Hospital Fund.
Art Director and Designer: Ellen Shapiro
Portrait Photographer: Mark Ferri

PAGE 117

Identity for "Channeling Children's Anger," a conference and public service television campaign for the Institute for Mental Health Initiatives.
Art Directors: Ellen Shapiro and Allen Kay
Designer and Illustrator: Terri Bogaards
Photographer: Peggy Barnett

PAGE 118

"Establishment Services Communication Guidelines" or American Express.
Art Director, Designer, and Copywriter: Ellen Shapiro

Directory of Manhattan restaurants welcoming the American Express® Card.
Art Director and Designer: Ellen Shapiro
Photographer: Peggy Barnett

PAGE 119

Clients and Designers, a book by Ellen Shapiro.
Art Director and Designer: Ellen Shapiro

Logo for "Bouncing Back," an educational program sponsored by the Institute for Mental Health Initiatives.
Art Directors and Designers: Ellen Shapiro and Allen Kay

PAGE 120

Ad campaign for Century Time Ltd., makers of hand-faceted, sapphire watches.
Art Director, Designer, and Copywriter: Ellen Shapiro

Capabilities brochure for International Typeface Corporation.
Art Director and Designer: Ellen Shapiro

PAGE 121

Identity guidelines for Schlumberger Ltd., multinational oil drilling and exploration corporation.
Art Director and Designer: Ellen Shapiro
Photographers: Robb Kendrick and Sepp Seitz

Annual report for Electro-Biology, Inc., manufacturer of electronic bone-healing equipment.
Art Director and Designer: Ellen Shapiro
Designer: Donald W. Burg
Illustrator: Javier Romero
Photographers: Michael Melford and Richard Frank

LORI SIEBERT

PAGE 122

Portrait Photographer: Bray Ficken Photography

Materials for the "Hewlett-Packard Peripherals Developers Conference '92."
Art Director: Lori Siebert
Designer: Barb Raymond
Client: Hewlett-Packard

PAGE 123

Brochure for Jack Rouse Associates.
Art Director: Lori Siebert
Designers: Lori Siebert, Lisa Ballard, and David Carroll

"City Shapes" edition of *Printing by Design.*
Art Director: Lori Siebert
Designer: Lori Siebert
Photographer: Jeff Friedman
Client: Sidney Printing Works

PAGE 124

Poster on communication for CompuServe.
Art Director: Lori Siebert
Designers: David Carroll and Lori Siebert, with Sive Associates

PAGE 125

Poster, notecard, and stationery line entitled "Wild about the World."
Art Director: Lori Siebert
Designers: David Carroll and Lori Siebert
Client: Good Nature Designs

Stationery for Jean Cecil Gilliam, Inc., architect and interior designer.
Art Director: Lori Siebert
Designer: Lisa Ballard

PAGE 126

"Formations" brochure for Formica Corporation.
Art Director: Lori Siebert
Designers: Lori Siebert and Lisa Ballard
Photographer: Jeff Kauck

Identity system for retailer Rags 2 Riches.
Art Director: Lori Siebert
Designers: Lori Siebert and Dana Beverly
Illustrator: Dana Beverly
Photographer: Michael Wilson

PAGE 127

Posters for the Cincinnati Symphony and Pops Orchestras.
Art Director: Lori Siebert
Designer: Lori Siebert
Photonics/Digitized Imager: Alan Brown

PAGE 128

Series of notecards for Good Nature Designs.
Art Director: Lori Siebert
Designers: Lori Siebert, Lisa Ballard, David Carroll, and Barb Raymond

Annual report for Mercy Health System.
Art Director: Lori Siebert
Designers: Lori Siebert, Barb Raymond, and Lisa Ballard
Illustrator: Lisa Ballard
Photographer: Gordon Morioka

PAGE 129

Brochure for FINIS, a post production company for film and video.
Art Director: Lori Siebert
Designers: Lisa Ballard and Lori Siebert
Illustrator: Lori Siebert

Stationery system for FINIS.
Art Director: Lori Siebert
Designers and Illustrators: Lisa Ballard and Lori Siebert

CATHERINE LAM SIU-HUNG

PAGE 130

Christmas card for Triumph International (HK) Ltd.
Art Director and Designer: Catherine Lam Siu-hung
Design Firm: Triumph International (HK) Ltd.

PAGE 131

Poster for volunteer gathering of the Kwun Tong Community Centre.
Art Director and Designer: Catherine Lam Siu-hung
Illustrator: Catherine Lam Siu-hung
Design Firm: Cat Lam Design Co.
Client: Hong Kong Caritas Community Centre, Ngau Tau Kok

Poster for youth sex education.
Art Director and Designer: Catherine Lam Siu-hung
Illustrator: Catherine Lam Siu-hung
Design Firm: Cat Lam Design Co.
Client: Hong Kong Caritas Community Centre, Aberdeen

PAGE 132

Horoscope icons for Art Gallery.
Art Director and Designer: Catherine Lam Siu-hung
Illustrator: Catherine Lam Siu-hung
Design Firm: Cat Lam Design Co.

PAGE 133

Horoscope postcards for Art Gallery.
Art Director and Designer: Catherine Lam Siu-hung
Illustrator: Catherine Lam Siu-hung
Design Firm: Cat Lam Design Co.

Invitation to HOM fashion show.
Art Director and Designer: Catherine Lam Siu-hung
Design Firm: Triumph International (HK) Ltd.
Client: Triumph International (HK) Ltd.

PAGE 134

Promotional poster for STAR TV, China.
Art Directors: Bethany Bunnell and Joe Kurzer
Designer: Catherine Lam Siu-hung
Design Firm: STAR TV Creative Services
Client: STAR TV

PAGE 135

"Morrison" brochure for Tsang Fook Piano Company.
Art Director and Designer: Catherine Lam Siu-hung
Design Firm: Cat Lam Design Co.

Desktop calendar for Tsang Fook Piano Company.
Art Director and Designer: Catherine Lam Siu-hung
Illustrator: Catherine Lam Siu-hung
Copywriter: Timothy Leung Chun Ming

PAGE 136

Wedding card.
Art Director and Designer: Catherine Lam Siu-hung
Design Firm: Cat Lam Design Co.
Client: Catherine Lam Siu-hung

Invitation for "On Democracy," an educational campaign.
Art Director and Designer: Catherine Lam Siu-hung
Illustrator: Catherine Lam Siu-hung
Design Firm: Cat Lam Design Co.
Client: Hong Kong Caritas Community Centre, Aberdeen

PAGE 137

Promotional material for a children's carnival.
Art Director and Designer: Catherine Lam Siu-hung
Illustrator: Catherine Lam Siu-hung

LESLIE SMOLAN

PAGE 138

Portrait Photographer: Rodney Smith

The Hat Book, a self-promotion by Carbone Smolan Associates.
Photographer: Rodney Smith

PAGE 139

Identity and guest amenities for Rafael Group/Rafael Hotel.
Photographer: Grant Peterson
Interior Designer: Chhada Siembieda & Partners

PAGE 140

Product design and brand identity for Primis, McGraw-Hill's customized textbook series.
Photographer: George Kamper
Cover Illustrator: Chris Gall

PAGE 141

Product styling for Dansk dinnerware.
Photographer: Irvin Blitz
Industrial Designer: Lorenzo Porcelli

PAGE 142

Packaging, identity, and ads for Springer's, a clothing retailer.
Photographer: Grant Peterson

PAGE 143

Visitor information system and signage for The Grand Louvre.
Photographers: Philippe de Potestad and George Kamper
Architect: I.M. Pei, Pei Cobb Freed & Partners

PAGE 144

Advertising campaign for FPG Stock Photo.
Photographers: Tom Kelley and Hy Peskin

"The Challenge of a New Environment" cover for Merrill Lynch.
Illustrator: Mark Penberthy

PAGE 145

Catalog cover for STA 100 Show (now American Center for Design).
Cover Illustrator: Leslie Smolan

Elementary textbook and marketing materials for Houghton-Mifflin's The Literature Experience.
Photographer: George Kamper
Cover Illustrators: Tedd Arnold, Marilee Heyer, and Maurice Sendak

DEBORAH SUSSMAN

PAGE 146

Portrait Photographer: Burton Pritzker

Three-dimensional model of a pedestrian entry portal at Sherman Oaks Galleria, a mixed-use development.
Principal: Deborah Sussman
Associate: Robert Cordell
Senior Designer: Lance Glover
Photographer: Annette Del Zoppo Photography
Client: Galleria Joint Venture

PAGE 147

Serpentine fence commemorating past Olympic Games.
Principals: Deborah Sussman and Paul Prejza
Associates: Mark Nelsen, Debra Valencia, and Scott Cuyler
Photographer: ADZ Productions
Client: Los Angeles 1984 Olympics Organizing Committee

Public food facility, one of many venues created for the 1984 Olympic Games in Los Angeles.
Principals: Deborah Sussman and Paul Prejza
Associates: Mark Nelsen, Debra Valencia, and Scott Cuyler
Photographer: ADZ Productions
Client: Los Angeles 1984 Olympics Organizing Committee

Detail of mural in the Athletic Village at the University of California at Los Angeles.
Principals: Deborah Sussman and Paul Prejza
Associates: Mark Nelsen, Debra Valencia, and Scott Cuyler
Photographer: ADZ Productions
Client: Los Angeles 1984 Olympics Organizing Committee

PAGE 148

Stationery for The Gas Company.
Principal: Deborah Sussman
Associate: Debra Valencia
Project Manager: Trent Fleming
Senior Designers: Ron Romero and Maureen Nishikawa
Photographer: Craig McMillan
Client: Southern California Gas Company

Triple chandelier application of The Gas Company logo.
Principal: Deborah Sussman
Associate: Scott Cuyler
Project Manager: Trent Fleming
Photographer: Nick Merrick, Hedrich-Blessing
Client: Southern California Gas Company

PAGE 149

Main entrance showing logo, signage, and exterior color of New Orlean's Aquarium of the Americas.
Principal: Deborah Sussman
Associate: Mark Nelsen
Senior Designer: Chuck Milhaupt
Photographer: Timothy Hursley
Client: Audubon Zoological Institute

Interior of the corporate headquarters and showroom of Hasbro, Inc., a toy manufacturer.
Principal: Deborah Sussman
Associates: Mark Nelsen and Fernando Vazquez
Photographer: Bo Parker

PAGE 150

Detail of "Headdress" sculpture in the interior of Chicago Place.
Principal: Deborah Sussman
Associate: Fernando Vazquez
Senior Designer: Lance Glover
Photographer: Fernando Vazquez
Client: Brookfield Devlopment (formerly BCE Development Properties)

Interior of Chicago Place, a retail center.
Principal: Deborah Sussman
Associate: Fernando Vazquez
Senior Designer: Lance Glover
Photographer: Timothy Hursley
Collaborator: Skidmore, Owings & Merrill
Client: Brookfield Devlopment (formerly BCE Development Properties)

PAGE 151

Exterior colors at The Citadel, a mixed-use development of a historical tire factory.
Principals: Deborah Sussman and Paul Prejza
Associates: Fernando Vazquez and Scott Cuyler
Senior Designer: Holly Hampton
Photographer: © Jeff Goldberg, ESTO
Client: Trammel-Crow Development

Architectural design with color, graphics, and signage at East Arcade, retail center of The Citadel.
Principals: Deborah Sussman and Paul Prejza
Associates: Fernando Vazquez and Scott Cuyler
Senior Designer: Holly Hampton
Photographer: © Jeff Goldberg, ESTO
Client: Trammel-Crow Development

Plaza, retail center of The Citadel.
Principals: Deborah Sussman and Paul Prejza
Associates: Fernando Vazquez and Scott Cuyler
Senior Designer: Holly Hampton
Photographer: Jeremy Samuelson
Client: Trammel-Crow Development

PAGE 152

EuroDisney bus.
Principal: Deborah Sussman
Associate: Robert Cordell
Senior Designers: Dan Evans and Maureen Nishikawa
Photographer: Luc Boeguy, Archipress
Client: EuroDisney S.C.A.

Freeway sign, part of a signage program for Walt Disney World.
Principal: Deborah Sussman
Associate: Robert Cordell
Senior Designer: Scott Cuyler
Photographer: Timothy Hursley
Client: Disney Development Company

Directional sign for Walt Disney World.
Principal: Deborah Sussman
Associate: Robert Cordell
Senior Designer: Scott Cuyler
Photographer: Timothy Hursley
Client: Disney Development Company

PAGE

Identity program for EuroDisney.
Principal: Deborah Sussman
Associate: Robert Cordell
Senior Designers: Dan Evans and Maureen Nishikawa
Photographer: Annette Del Zoppo Photography
Client: EuroDisney S.C.A.

1991 annual report for EuroDisney.
Principal: Deborah Sussman
Associate: Robert Cordell
Senior Designers: Dan Evans and Maureen Nishikawa
Photographer: Annette Del Zoppo Photography
Client: EuroDisney S.C.A.

ROSMARIE TISSI

PAGE 154

Ad for a Belgian advertising magazine called *Tips*.
Art Director and Designer: Rosmarie Tissi

PAGE 155

Poster for Merce Cunningham Dance Company.
Art Director and Designer: Rosmarie Tissi

PAGE 156

Portfolio for Offset, a printer.
Art Director and Designer: Rosmarie Tissi

Logo for Kupferschmid, a paper dealer.
Art Director and Designer: Rosmarie Tissi

PAGE 157

Portfolio of posters given as a promotional gift by Reprotechnik Koten AG, a printer.
Art Director and Designer: Rosmarie Tissi

PAGE 158

Human rights poster for "Artis 89."
Art Director and Designer: Rosmarie Tissi

PAGE 159

Program poster, introducing new logo, for Theater 11.
Art Director and Designer: Rosmarie Tissi

Summer theater poster.
Art Director and Designer: Rosmarie Tissi

One of a series of banknote designs.
Art Director and Designer: Rosmarie Tissi

PAGE 160

Ad for Englercomputergrafik, a computer graphics firm.
Art Director and Designer: Rosmarie Tissi

Poster for Englersatz AG, typesetters.
Art Director and Designer: Rosmarie Tissi

Water wheel logo for a flour mill.
Art Director and Designer: Rosmarie Tissi

PAGE 161

Poster for a series of concerts in the park.
Art Director and Designer: Rosmarie Tissi

LYNN TRICKETT

PAGE 162

Mail order catalogs for Alphabet Soup, an antiques dealer.
Art Directors and Designers: Lynn Trickett, Brian Webb, and Jan Moscowitz

PAGE 163

"Lifestyle" brochure for Dorma, a bed linens company.
Art Directors and Designers: Lynn Trickett, Brian Webb, and Avril Broadley
Photographers: Bill Batten and Sandra Lousada

Series of stamps entitled "Memories" for Royal Mail.
Art Directors and Designers: Lynn Trickett, Brian Webb, and Andrew Thomas
Photographer: Carol Sharp

PAGE 164

Identity for a line of cosmetics for young girls.
Art Directors and Designers: Lynn Trickett, Brian Webb, and Debbie Tiso
Illustrator: Kathie Felstead
Client: Boots the Chemists

PAGE 165

Packaging for a line of children's felt-tipped pens for WH Smith Ltd.
Art Directors and Designers: Lynn Trickett, Brian Webb, and Suzanne Evans
Illustrator: Brian Grimwood

Packaging for "Creative Play," a series of activities for children.
Art Directors and Designers: Lynn Trickett, Brian Webb, and Suzanne Evans
Illustrator: Jason Ford

PAGE 166

"Green Issue," a series of environmental stamps using children's winning illustrations.
Art Directors and Designers: Lynn Trickett, Brian Webb, and Andrew Thomas
Illustrators: Christopher Hall, Lewis Fowler, Sarah Jo Warren, and Alice Newton-Mold

A Royal Mail Christmas book titled *Lickety Stick.*
Art Directors and Designers: Lynn Trickett, Brian Webb, and Sarah Mattinson
Stamp Illustrator: Dan Fern
Copywriter: Neil Mattingley

PAGE 167

The Shoeshine Outfit, a line of Christmas gifts for men.
Art Directors and Designers: Lynn Trickett, Brian Webb, and Andrew Thomas
Illustrator: Mark Thomas
Client: Boots the Chemists

"I Am a Doughnut" calendar for screen printers, designers, and illustrators.
Art Directors and Designers: Lynn Trickett, Brian Webb, and Steve Edwards
Illustrators: Lawrence Zeegan, Jeff Fisher, Michael Bartalos, Dan Fern, Philippe Weisbecker, Toby Morrison, Marion Deuchars, George Hardie, Peter Blake, Isabelle Dervaux, Andrew Kulman, and Ian Beck
Client: Augustus Martin and Trickett & Webb Ltd.

PAGE 168

A how-to-landscape brochure for Highgate Garden Centre.
Art Directors and Designers: Lynn Trickett, Brian Webb, and Ian Moscowitz
Illustrator: George Hardie
Copywriter: Neil Mattingley

Weather Report Christmas book for Royal Mail.
Art Directors and Designers: Lynn Trickett, Brian Webb, and Sarah Mattinson
Stamp Illustrator: Andrew Davidson
Copywriter: Lynn Trickett

PAGE 169

Calendar for photographer Robert Dowling.
Art Directors and Designers: Lynn Trickett, Brian Webb, and Avril Broadley
Photographer: Robert Dowling

Expressions, a line of recycled writing paper for WH Smith Ltd.
Art Directors and Designers: Lynn Trickett, Brian Webb, and Avril Broadley

SUSANNA VALLEBONA

PAGE 170

Signage for S.O.S. Infanzia, an organization to assist abused children.
Art Director and Designer: Susanna Vallebona

PAGE 171

Book covers for Elio Sellino Editore.
Art Director and Designer: Susanna Vallebona

Poster for Tecnavia, photo transmission technology.
Art Director and Designer: Susanna Vallebona

PAGE 172

Corporate identity for publisher Elio Sellino Editore.
Art Director and Designer: Susanna Vallebona

Wedding invitation for Sergio Lochis.
Art Director and Designer: Susanna Vallebona

PAGE 173

Labels for a line of flavored vodkas by Lazza.
Art Director and Designer: Susanna Vallebona

Label for Lazza amaretto liqueur.
Art Director and Designer: Susanna Vallebona

PAGE 174

Event logo and brochure for a golf meeting sponsored by S.T. Dupont.
Art Director and Designer: Susanna Vallebona

Trademark for Consulting Milano, a building company.
Art Director and Designer: Susanna Vallebona

Arcana Editrice logo for a series of books with CD's.
Art Director and Designer: Susanna Vallebona

PAGE 175

Ad campaign for S.O.S. Infanzia, an organization to assist abused children.
Art Director and Designer: Susanna Vallebona

Giraffa Trading, a magazine for boys by producers of toys.
Art Director and Designer: Susanna Vallebona

PAGE 176

Promotional poster for "Meie Assicurazioni," an annual celebration.
Art Director and Designer: Susanna Vallebona

Brochure for Tecnavia, photo transmission technology.
Art Director and Designer: Susanna Vallebona

PAGE 177

Poster for "Centro S. Fedele" competition.
Art Director and Designer: Susanna Vallebona

NANCY WILLIAMS

PAGE 178

Annual report and accounts for Post Office Counters.
Art Director: Nancy Williams
Designers: Laura Heard, Susan Howells, Martin Cox, and Nancy Williams

PAGE 179

Looseleaf brochure for Paternoster Square development project.
Art Director: Nancy Williams
Designers: Richard Scholey and Nancy Williams

Portfolio containing limited-edition horticultural prints presented at the opening of the Chelsea Flower Show.
Art Director: Nancy Williams
Designers: Nancy Williams and Laura Heard
Client: Olympia & York Canary Wharf

PAGE 180

Prospectus for Inchbald School of Design.
Art Director: Nancy Williams
Designers: Bob Mytton, Tim Webb Jenkins, and Stephen Taylor

PAGE 181

Stationery for Nicholas Gill Associates, architects.
Art Director: Phoa Kia Boon
Designers: Phoa Kia Boon and Nancy Williams

PAGE 182

Packaging for a wool blanket by Boots.
Art Director: Nancy Williams
Designers: Peter Thompson and Nancy Williams

Book design for *Ehrets Flowering Plants.*
Art Director: Nancy Williams
Designers: Nancy Williams and Francis Hartog
Clients: Webb & Bower, and Victoria and Albert Museum

PAGE 183

Brochure for Roughton and Fenton, engineers.
Art Director: Nancy Williams
Designer: Albert Kueh

Project brochure for Olympia & York's Canary Wharf development.
Art Director: Nancy Williams
Designers: Richard Scholey, Nancy Williams, and Francis Hartog

PAGE 184

Brochure for TTSP, architects.
Art Director: Phoa Kia Boon
Designers: Nancy Williams and Laura Heard

Call for entries for a student awards competition.
Art Director: Nancy Williams
Designer: Richard Bonner Morgan
Clients: D&AD and Post Office

PAGE 185

Wine labels for France Vin Limited.
Designer: Nancy Williams

Corporate brochure for Extel.
Art Directors and Designers: Phoa Kia Boon and Nancy Williams

About the Selection Process

Supon Design Group's own committee of design professional's selected the twenty-three designers and hundreds of projects featured herein. The highly selective process began with the committee's nomination of sixty designers from a dozen countries. All respected and award-winning, these women ranged from freelancers at one-person studios to partners at the world's leading agencies. Each was invited to send materials for consideration; and most all complied. The committee then made its final selection. In addition to talent and quality of work (both obvious prerequisites), there were several criteria for inclusion. Foremost among these was diversity —

in style, type of work, geographic base, and size and specialty of the firm. Above all, however, the committee sought those pieces which would aptly represent the high caliber of work in today's marketplace.

As an industry insider, you are in a perfect position to nominate designers for inclusion in our various upcoming publications. Just complete the following form, and send it with ten samples of the designer's best work. (Of course, the designer may be you, if you are so inclined.) Supon Design Group will happily consider all work submitted. Materials cannot be returned, and all decisions will be final.

Nomination form for upcoming publications

Designer's Name_____ Firm_____

Address_____

_____Country_____

Telephone_____ Fax_____

Your name *(if different than designer's name above)*_____ Firm_____

Address_____

_____Country_____

Telephone_____ Fax_____

Please make a copy of this form, complete it, and send it along with ten samples of the designer's best work to:

Supon Design Group, Inc., International Book Division
1000 Connecticut Avenue, NW, Suite 415
Washington, DC 20036 USA

On the outside of all international submissions, please write "Material for Contest Entry / No Commercial Value."

Supon Design Group Staff from left to right: *Linda Klinger, Wayne Kurie, Supon Phornirunlit, Andy Dolan, Dianne Cook, Rick Heffner, and Pica, the Wonder Dog.*

SUPON DESIGN GROUP

A five-year-old studio located in Washington, D.C., Supon Design Group specializes in a wide range of graphic arts. Owner and Art Director Supon Phornirunlit heads the company, and is responsible for managing its growth. The studio's International Book Division authors several publications annually on the subject of graphic design. Since its inception, the studio has been featured in numerous international publications. These include *How's Business Annual*, the American Institute of Graphic Art's *Journal*, *Designers' Self-Image*, and Asia's *Media Delite*. In the past five years, Supon Design Group has earned over 250 awards from every major design organization. *Communication Arts*, *Graphis*, AIGA, Type Directors Club, *Studio Magazine*, New York Art Director's Club, and *Print* are among those that have recognized the firm's talents. Samples of Supon Design Group's work have been exhibited in England, Germany, Israel, Japan, Thailand, and the United States.

DATE DUE

NOV. 26. 2007		

Demco